Lyman Haynes Low

# Catalogue of a large and interesting collection of mediaeval and modern copper coins

## modern copper coins

Third sale 12/1883

Lyman Haynes Low

**Catalogue of a large and interesting collection of mediaeval and modern copper coins**
*Third sale 12/1883*

ISBN/EAN: 9783741177989

Manufactured in Europe, USA, Canada, Australia, Japa

Cover: Foto ©Lupo / pixelio.de

Manufactured and distributed by brebook publishing software (www.brebook.com)

Lyman Haynes Low

# Catalogue of a large and interesting collection of mediaeval and modern copper coins

# THIRD SALE.

—————

# CATALOGUE

OF A

LARGE AND INTERESTING COLLECTION

OF

## Mediæval and Modern Copper Coins,

### FOR SALE AT FIXED PRICES,

BY

## LYMAN H. LOW,

OF

# B. WESTERMANN & CO.,

IMPORTERS AND DEALERS IN ANCIENT, MEDIÆVAL
AND MODERN COINS, MEDALS AND TOKENS;

ALSO,

## NUMISMATIC PUBLICATIONS,

### 838 BROADWAY, NEW YORK.

—————

DECEMBER, 1883.

# PREFACE.

The line of Copper here offered is most remarkable, and has, as to rarities, never been equalled in this country. Nearly every piece is either rare or in fine condition, and is, in many instances, catalogued for the first time.

A large portion of these coins are from my own cabinet, and have been for years highly prized by me as the gems of my collection.

They were obtained with great difficulty, and in many instances it is exceedingly doubtful if they could ever be duplicated.

As an opportunity to complete sets which many collectors already own, *all but the rare ones*, the present cannot be excelled. Read the following pages carefully and you will find the missing rarity there.

As heretofore, I have sedulously avoided an over-description as to condition, and collectors will, in every instance, find the coin fully equal to my representations.

My next sale, which will occur in March, will be a continuation of the present and will be made up of coins not previously described in my catalogues, being, as in this instance, largely from my own cabinet.

LYMAN H. LOW.

# CATALOGUE.

1 **Amersfort**, *Jetton.* Eight letters in mon. crowned. *Rer.*, PALLADIU AM'S-FORT 1664 on a label. Unc. 22.   .50

2 **Ancona** (1798–99), 2 *Baiocchi;* Fasces. REP. ROM. ANCONA. *Rer.*, DVE | BAIOC | CIII. Broad milled rim. Fine. 22. .75

3 **Antigua**, 1836, *Farthing.* Tree, dividing date. Good. .60

4 **Aquila**, *Innocent VIII.*, 1485–86. INNOCENTIVS P. P. VIII. Two keys crossed. *Rec.*, AQVILANA LIBERTAS. Eagle. *Quattrino.* Good. 12.   .30

5 —— *Chas. VIII.*, 1495. CAROLVS REX, F. R. R. Three fleur-de-lis in crowned shield. *Rev.*, CIVITAS AQVILANA. Cross and eagle. *Cavallo.* Pierced, otherwise good. 12. .18

6 **Argau**, 1816, 1 *Rappen.* Good. 10.   .15

7 **Armata and Morea**, *Cassetto* (or 2 *Soldi*). The Venetian lion. Good. 18.   .18

8 **Arnheim**, *Doit.* MONE T. ARNHEM IN GELRIA. Fair. .15 .25

9 **Artois**, *Philip III.* (1636), *Liard.* Bust. *Rer.*, Arms crowned. Poor. 18.   .15

10 **Audenade** (1582), *Sol.* Lion in four-barred shield, above, a gothic A. *Rer.*, Blank. A necessity piece in tin. Lozenge shaped. Good. 9x9.   .75

11 —— Another for 10 *Liards*, with SPES NVA DEVS 1582 and A crowned. Counterstamped A. Tin. Good. 14x14 1.00

12 **Augsburg** (Bishopric), *Heinrich von Knöringen* Arms, a shield with a plain field, divided in centre by a single Pale; above, 1622. *Rev.*, 1 | KREIT | ZER. Fair. 11.   .20

13 - —— (City), 1551. Date divided by a large fur-cone (the arms of the city). *Rer.*, a torch. Chimney-sweepers' token. Good. 17.   .25

14 —— 1608. Date divided as above. *Rer.*, CCCC—XX. 420th *Gulden.* Fair. 8.   .18

15 —— 1622. Date divided as in No. 13. *Rer.*, 1 | KREI | ZER. Good. 10.   .15

16 —— 1758. Conc. *Rer.*, date divided by a St. Andrew's cross. *Heller.* Octagonal. 8x8. Fine.   .18

17 —— 1758. Conc. *Rev.*, II | PFENNING | STADT MYNZ. Good. 14.   .15

18 —— 1762. 1 *Pfg. Rer.*, as above. Fair. 12.   .12

19 —— 1780. 1 *Pfg. Rer.*, as above, but in curved lines. Fair. 12.   .12

20 —— 1786. *Heller.* Fair. 9.   .12

21 **Austria**, *Francis I.*, 1816, ¼, ½, and 1 *Krzr.*; 1848, 2 *Krzr.*, all with mint mark A (Vienna). Red, uncir. 4 pcs. .35

22 —— 1881. ⁵⁄₁₀ and 1 *Krzr.* Red, uncir. 2 pcs.   .15

23 **Avignon**, *Urban VIII.*, 1637, *Quattrino.* Bust. *Rer.*, three fleur-de lis. Poor. 13.   .12

24 **Baden**, *Leopold Carl*, 1852. ½ *Krzr.* Head, r. Red, uncir. .15

25 **Baltimore.** An anchor, with a star above and at either side. *Rer.*, Fasces, bow and arrows crossed, between two cornucopias. Brass. Good. 11. .50

26 ——— Similar, in copper, struck with a collar. Good. 14. .35
[Note:—The above two numbers have generally been attributed to Trinidad. I have possessed Tokens of this city, having either side of these pieces as a reverse, therefore I believe them to be Baltimore Mules.]

27 **Barbadoes,** 1788, *Penny.* Negro with plumed head-dress. *Rer.*, Pineapple. Fair. 20. .35

28 ——— 1792, *Halfpenny. Rer.*, Neptune in his car. Fair. 16. .40

29 ——— Moses Tolanto, *Halfpenny* Token. Bale. *Rev.*, Barrel. Fair. 18. .25

30 **Barcelona,** *Philip IV.*, 1653. *Ardite.* The letters A—R(dite) separated by bust. *Rev.*, Arms. BARCINO CIVI(tas). Poor. 11. .12

31 ——— *Louis XIII.*, 1642, *Seiseno.* Bust. *Rev.*, similar to last. Fair. 14. .15

32 ——— *Louis XIV.*, 1649, *Seiseno.* Same type as preceding. Fair. 14. .15

33 ——— *Philip V.*, 1710, *Dinerillos.* Bust. Es VN DINER. *Rev.*, arms and date. Good. 9. .20

34 ——— *During French Occupation,* 1810. 4 *Quartos.* Arms without inscription. *Rev.*, "EN BARCELONA." Value in field. Good 18. .25

35 ——— 1808. 2 *Quartos.* Same type as last. Fair. 16. .40

36 ——— 1809. 1 *Quarto.* Same as preceding. Fair. 14. .60

37 ——— ½ *Quarto.* Without date or inscription. Arms. Value on *Rer.* Pierced near edge. Otherwise good. 12. .75

38 ——— *Ferd. VII.*, 1823. 6 *Quartos.* Arms of Castile and Leon crowned. *Rev.*, arms of the Province, crowned. Good. 20. .35

39 ——— 1823. 3 *Quartos.* Same type. Good. 17. .30

40 **Basel,** 1810. 1 *Rappen.* Good. 10. .15

41 **Bavaria.** *Max. I.*, 1598-1651. Arms without inscription. *Rer.*, I. (Pfg.) within a circle of dots. Fair. 7. .15

42 ——— *Max. Jos. II.*, 1765. *Heller.* Arms dividing the letters C(hur) B(ayern), date above. *Rev.*, 1 | HEL | LER | A | within lozenge. Good. 10. .15

43 ——— 1761. *Heller.* Arms dividing date within a lozenge. *Rev.*, As last. Good. 10. .15

44 ——— Max. John IV., 1806. 1 *Kreuzer.* Shield bearing lion and Imperial apple, within the arms of Bavaria. *Rer.*, value, date, &c. Struck at Hall, in Tyrol. Good. 16. .20

45 **Belgium,** *Leop. I.*, 1832. 10 *Centimes.* Uncir. 20. .25

46 **Bolivia,** 1878. 1 *Centavo.* REPUBLICA BOLIVIANA. *Rer.*, Value in wreath. Good. 13. .40

47 **Bologna,** (Bononia), *Clement VIII.*, 1592-1605. *Quattrino.* Bust. CLEMES VIII. PONT MAX. *Rev.*, arms. BONONIA DOGET. Good. 11. .35

48 ——— *Gregory XV.*, 1621. Arms. BONONIA DOGET. *Rer.*, Lion rampant l. behind ornamented shield bearing the numerals: MDCXXI; above, MEZZO BOLOGNINO. Good. 18. .50

49 ——— *Innocent XI.*, 1681. *Mezzo Bolognino.* Same type as last. Date in figures. Good. 18. .35

50 ——— *Alexander VIII.*, 1691. Same type and denomination as preceding. Fair. 18. .40

51 ——— *Innocent XII. Quattrino.* Lion holding a pole which carries a pennant. *Rer.*, BONO | NIA | DOGET | 1691. Good. 12. .18

52 ——— *Innocent XIII.* Type of No. 47. *Rev.*, Lion. r. paw resting on shield enclosing 1723 MEZZO BOLOGNINO. Fair. 18. .40

53 —— *Pius VI*, 1779. *Quattrino*. Papal arms. *Rev.*,
BONO | NIA | DOGET and date. Good. 14. .15
54 —— Same. 1796. Large lion l. standing upon one hind foot.
BONONIA DOGET; In ex BAIOCCHI 2. *Rev.*, PIVS | SEXTVS |
PONTIFEX | MAXIMVS | MDCCXCVI. Good. 24. .65
55 —— Same *Baiocco*. Fair. 21. .40
56 —— Same *M(ezzo) Bai(occo).*) Fair. 17. .30
57 —— Similar. 1796. *Quattrino*. Date in figures. Red unc.
14. .40
58 **Brabant,** *Philip II.,* 1583. *Liard.* Crowned head l. PHS.
D. G. HISP. Z REX. BRA. Date in ex. separated by a star.
(m. m. of Maestrecht). *Rev.*, arms crowned. DOMINVS MIHI
ADIVTOR. Fair. 17. .40
59 —— Same, (15) 87, *Liard,* the two figures of the date separated
by an open hand. (m. m. of Antwerp). Poor. 16. .25
60 —— Same (without date), *Liard.* Head l. PHS. D. G. HISP.
Z. REX. DVX. BRA. m. m. an open hand. *Rev.*,
crowned arms. PACE ET IVSTITIA. Good. 17. .40
61 —— Same (without date). *Demi Liard.* Heard r. *Rev..* arms
quartered by Jerusalem cross. Legend as on No. 58.
Poor. 15. .18
62 —— *Albert* and *Elizabeth*, 1608, *Liard.* Arms crowned. *Rev.*,
shield with 5-pointed star upon St. Andrew's cross, separating date; above, a crown; below, a fleece, ARCHI.
DVCES, AVST. DVC. BVR. E. B. Good. 16. .25
63 —— Same, 1615, *Demi Liard.* Similar to last. Fair. 14. .20
64 —— *Charles II.,* 1691, *Liard.* Arms crowned, date divided
by the crown. *Rev.*, crown between four shields in form
of cross. m. m. A head. (Brussels.) Fair. 16. .18
65 —— Same, 1696, *Demi Liard.* Crowned arms of Brabant
alone, date as above. *Rev.*, St. Andrew's cross. m. m.
of Antwerp. Good. 13. .20
66 —— *Maria Theresa*, *Liard.* Naked bust r. *Rev.*, AD | USUM
| BELGII AUSTR. 1744, m. m. the open hand. Good.
15. .20
67 —— Same, 1750 (2d coinage). *Double Liard.* Bust as before,
with necklace.of beads. *Rev.*, as last, but within wreath.
Fine. 17. .45
[Note.—The two above numbers are fine specimens of art by the celebrated Joseph Roettiers, indicated by the letter R. beneath Bust.]
68 —— Same. 1777 (3d Coinage.) *Liard.* Bust r. Head and
shoulders draped. *Rev.*, as preceding, m. m. of Brussels.
Unc. 14. .30
69 —— *Jos. II,* 1789. *Double Liard.* Bust r. Jos. II. D. G. R.
IMP. D. B. *Rev.*, same as No. 67. m. m. of Brussels.
Poor. 18. .12
70 —— *Francis II.;* 1793. *Double Liard.* Same type. Brussels.
Fine. 18. .25
71 **Buenos Ayres,** 1822. (During British occupation.) *Decimo.*
*Rev.*, has 3 scratches and a small portion of glue adher-
ing. Bronze proof. 15. .40
72 —— 1830, 20 *Decimos,* Phœnix, Red unc. Thick. 20. .45
73 **Bulgaria,** *Alexander.* 10 *Stotinki.* Arms draped and surmounted by the Princes' crown. Inscription in Russian.
*Rev.*, 10 C A Н T N M 1880. ESSAI. Proof. Has been
somewhat handled, but is unstained. 19. .75
74 **Brandenburg** (Province), *Fred. II.,* 1752, 3 *Pfg.* F. R. in
ornamented monogram, crowned; the letter A divides date.
Good. 17. .18
75 —— Same, 1755. 1 *Pfg.* Good. 12. .10
76 —— (Margravate) *Chris. Fred. Chas. Alex.,* 1752. 1 *Pfg.* The
Brandenburg eagle with shield upon breast, within a
crowned shield. BRANDENBURG A SCHEIDE-NUNZE, date
in ex. *Rev.*, EIN | PFEN- | NING. Good. 13. .20

77 **Breda,** 1625. Arms, 3 small crosses in saltire in shield, separating 1—S(ol). *Rev.*, blank lozenge-shaped, 9x9. Fine. .75

[Note.—This is a piece of necessity, struck during the siege of the city by the Spaniards under Spinola.]

78 **Bremen,** 1841, *Half Groten.* Arms a key within crowned shield. FREIS HANSESTADT BREMEN. *Rev.*, value and date. Fine. 13. .20

79 **Bronkhorst,** *John II.*, 1588-1617, *Liard.* Bust r. JOES COMES D. BRONET. *Rev.*, crowned Arms. IN GRON. BAR. I. B. ET R. Poor. 13. .20

80 **Brunswick Luneburg,** *Ernst. Aug.*, 1692. 1 *Pfg*. E. A. in crowned mon. *Rev.*, Value and date. Good. 13. .15

81 —— *Fred. Wm.*, 1814. 2 *Pfg.* F. W. in crowned mon.; beneath, in small letters the initials of Fred. Ritter, director of the mint at Brunswick, 1814-1829. *Rev.*, value and date. Good. 16. .15

82 —— *William.* 2 *Pfg.* Galloping horse r. without legend. *Rev.*, 2 PFENNIGE 1852; beneath, small B. (Brumlin, m. m. in Brunswick.) Red uncirc. 14. .15

83 —— Same, 1852. *Pfennige.* Red uncirc. 12. .15

84 **Burgundy,** *Philip II.*, 1589, *Dinero,* Bust l. PHS REX CATOL. HISPAN. *Rev.*, COMES BVGVNDIE. Lion in field, date in legend. Fair. 14. .40

85 **Cabul,** Elephant. *Rev.*, Lion (early). Poor. 12. .15

86 **Camenz,** 3 *Pfg.* A wing supported at the shoulder by three pellets, in ex. 3 P F. *Rev.*, BONO | PVBL | CAM | 1622. Unc. 10. .35

87 —— *Pfg.* without date, the figure 1 at r. of wing. *Rev.*, incused. Unc. 8. .25

88 **Campen,** *Doit,* Castle with 3 towers. *Rev.*, CAM | PEN | 1644. Fair. 13. .25

89 **Candia** (under Venetian rule, 1632.) 60 *Tornesi. IOAN. KOPNHAIOS O. ΔΟΥΞ.* In field, *TOPNEΣIA EΞHNTA. Rev.*, the lion of St. Mark. *O A ΓIOΣ MOPKOΣ.* In ex. IIII. Good. 19. 1.00

90 **Carabobo,** (Venezuela). ¼ *Real.* Locomotive. CARABOBO YGUAL. *Rev.*, B. ANTICH | ¼ | REAL | 1881 |. Brass. Unc. 11. .18

91 **Carthegena,** (1812). 2 *Reals.* Indian seated beneath a tree. *Rev.*, ESTADO DE CARTHEGENA, VALE. DOS REALES. Rude. Poor. 18. .25

92 —— Same. *Rev.*, ¼ | ESTADO | DE CARTA | GENA | 1812. Good. 14. .35

93 **Casale,** (1630). Three fleur-de-lis in crowned shield separating F(loreni)— X. HORVM AIXILIO NON OPPRIMAR. *Rev.*, female seated l. within the outlines of a four-bastioned fortress. TENTATA SED INCORVPTA. In ex. CASALE. Battered, and pierced in centre. 20. 1.25

[Note.—The above, a piece of 10 Florins, was struck in Casale during its defence by Field-Marshall Toinace, against the Spaniards under Spinola. Neither the celebrated Rossi collection, nor that of Morbio, although both, almost exclusively of Italian coins, contained this piece in the above denomination, although those of 15 and 20 Florins were represented, realizing $10 each. Neumann, who seldom mentions rarity, in describing this piece, says " sehr selten " (*very rare.*)

94 **Castiglion,** *Francis Gonzaga,* 1593-1616, *Quattrino.* The letters F. G. in the field beneath a crown. PRINC CASTILLIONIS EC. *Rev.*, lion rampant, l. FIDES INCORRVPTA. Fair. 12. .30

95 ——— *Ferd. II.* 1680-1723. *Quattrino.* Bust r. FER. II.
PRIN. CAS. *Rev.*, MEDV | MAR | Ec. Fair. 11. .20
96 **Catalonia,** *Ferd. VI.* 1755. *Ardite.* Arms of Spain crowned
FERDINANDUS VI., D. G. *Rev.*, crowned shield of four
quarterings, 1st and 3d bearing Maltese cross. 2d and 4th
5 Pales. PRINCEPS CATALON. Fair. 12. .20
97 ——- Same. 1756. With large crowned shield bearing four
ales. Good. 12. .20
98 ——— *Ferd. VII.*, 1811. 6 *Quartos.* PRINCIP CATHAL. In
ex. VI. QUAR. Arms same as preceding number.
Good. 20. .30
99 ——— Same, 1810. 3 *Quartos.* *Rev.*, arms in oval shield.
Good. 16. .25
100 ——— Same, 1811. *Quarto.* (5 *Medios.*) Arms on both sides
in oval shield. Fair. 14. .35
101 ——— Same, 1813. *Quarto.* Shields, differing from all preceding. Fair. 13. .20
102 ——— Same, 1813. *Octavo.* Same *obverse* as No. 98. With-
OCHAVO. *Rev*, shield still dif. Good. 11. .30
103 ——— *Isabel II.* 1838. 6 *Quartos.* Same type as No. 98.
ISABEL 2A REYNA CONST. DE LAS E. *Rev.*, same as
No. 98. PRINCIP DE CATALUNA, In ex. 6 CUAR.
Good. 20. .35
104 ——— Same, 1837. 3 *Quartos.* *Rev.*, arms in oval shield.
Good. 17. .25
105 **Cattaro,** (City in Dalmatia under Venetian rule. 1420—1638
*Quattrino.* Saint standing separating .F--P. (Fran-
cisco Pisani Rector in Cattaro. 1548-49.) S(anctus)
TRIFONS CATARI. *Rev.* lion of St. Mark. S. MARCVS
VENETVS. Good. 10. .35
106 **Catorce** (Mexico), 1822, FONDOS PUBLICOS In ex. ¼ (Real).
*Rev.*, DE CATORCE. In field eagle perched upon the
Maguey plant. Good. 14. 2.75
[Note.—As far as I can learn this coin has heretofore been unde-
scribed. It is the only specimen I have ever met with.]
107 **Cayenne,** Three fleur-de-lis beneath a crown. LOUIS XVI.
R. DE FR. ET DE NAV. *Rev.*, COLONIE DE CAYENNE.
In field, 2 SOUS. 1789. m. m. A. (Paris). Thick
planchet of *pure copper.* Good. 15. .50
I never met with another.
108 **Chihuahua,** Indian with bow and arrow. ESTADO SOBE-
RANO DE CHIHUAHUA. *Rev.*, ¼ (Real). 1833 within
heavy palm wreath. Fair. 16. .25
109 ——— Same. 1834. .25
110 ——— Same. 1846. ESTADO LIBRE DE CHIHUAHUA. *Rev.*,
¼ (Real). Good. 16. .35
111 ——— Same. 1855. ESTADO DE CHIHUAHUA. *Rev.*, ¼ (Real).
Fair. 16. .25
112 ——— Same. E. CHIHA. LIBERTAD. Liberty seated. *Rev.*,
¼ | DE REAL | 1860. Good. 19. .35
113 **Clausthal,** *John William. Schlemon.* mint master, 1753-88.
*Jetton* CONSILIO & FORTUNA. Gaming implements. 1
W S in ex. *Rev.*, OMNIA CUM PONDERE NUMERO & MEN-
SURA. Justice holding plumb and scales. Good. 16. .18
114 ——— Same, *Jetton.* Legend as reverse of last. 1 W S in
ex. Female standing holding scales and cornucopia.
*Rev.*, FORTUNA VARIABILIS. Naked female standing
upon a rock in the open sea. Good. 16. .18
115 ——— *Henry Benhorst,* mint master, 1674-1711. *Jetton* QVIES-
CAM ET QVIESCERE FACIAM. Dove with olive branch
soaring above the clouds. *Rev.*, RESPONDENT INTIMA
QVANTO. Scales, etc., upon a platform. Good. 18. .18

116 **Cologne**, M(AX) F(RED) in crowned mon. *Rev.*, ¼ | STUBER | 1766 | I. K. Red, unc. 14. .18

117 **Corfu**, *Gazetto*. S. MARCVS VEN. in ex. II. *Rev.*, CORFV | CEFALON | ZANTE. Good. 17. .60

118 **Correggio**, *Camillus Fabricius*, 1580–97. *Soldo*. S. QVIR PRO. CIVIT CORRIGLE. Bust of St. Quirinus I. *Rev.*, SVB VMBRA ALARVM TVARVM. Eagle crowned. Poor. 12. . 5

119 —— Same, *Quattrino*. SIRVS AVSTR CORR. PRIN. Bust I. *Rev.*, SVB VMBRA ALARVM TVARVM. Eagle. Poor. 9. .15

120 **Corsica**, *Pascal Puoli*. Small bust I. in crowned shield. *Rev.*, 4 | SOLDI | 1766 | . Good. 14. .60

121 —— Same. Hat on a pole. *Rev.*, 1 | SOLDO | 1768. Fair. 11. .40

122 **Cyprus**, *James* I., 1382. *Cavallo*. JACOBVS RAIA. Lion rampant I. *Rev.*, X. RVSALE. Fair. 12. ·40

123 —— Obsidional. PRO REGNI CYPRII, PRESSIDIO. In the field the lion of St. Mark, beneath which is date 1570. *Rev.*. VENETORV | FIDE INVI | OLABILIS- | BISANTI | F. Small cherub above. Good. 17. .75

124 **Dalmatia**, *Domenico Contarini*, 1659–75. *Gazzetto*. SAN MARC VEN. In ex. II (Soldi). *Rev.*, DALMA(tia) | ET | ALBAN(ia). Fair. 18. .18

125 —— *Soldo*. S. MARC V. in ex. I. *Rev.*, DALM | ET | ALB. Fair. 13. .40

126 **Danzig**. Arms two Maltese crosses within a shield, supported by two lions. In ex. 1809. *Rev.*, DANZIGER KUPFER MUENZE. In field EIN GROSCHEN. Good. 13. .15

127 —— Same. Arms crowned, dividing 18——08. *Rev.*, 1 | SCHILLING. In ex. two branches crossed. Fair. 11. .15

128 **Daventer**. Obsidional. VRGEN NECESS DAVEN, 30 Oc.(tober) (15) 78. In field eagle. *Rev.*, S(ols) IIII. Good. 22. .80

129 —— Same. S(ols) II. Good. 18. .60

130 —— Same. S(ols) I. Good. 16. .60

131 —— Same. S(ol) P [¼]. Good. 14. .60
[Note.—The four preceding numbers are counterstamped with an eagle.]

132 **Demarary**. Geo. III., 1813. *Stirer*. Unc. A beautiful light olive. 22. .40

133 **Denmark**, *Fred. III*. F. 3 in crowned mon. DOMIN PROVID. *Rev.*, I | SOSLING | DANSKE | 1651. Good. 13. .25

134 —— *Christian V.*, 1670–99. Obsidional. The figure 5 within a large C, crowned, separating 8—S D (Shilling Danske). *Rev.*, blank Good Of rude workmanship. 19x20. 2.50
[Note.—These pieces are said to have been issued on the 1st day of May. 1677, by the Danish General Meerheim, who was at that time besieging the City of Christians adt.]

135 *Fred. VI.*, ¹⁄₈ *Rigsbank daler*. Arms of Denmark, Norway and Sweden in a crowned oval shield. *Rev.*, 2 RIGSBANK SHILLING. 1818. Fair. 19. .18

136 —— ₉⁄₆ *Rigsbankdaler*. *Rev.*, 1 | RIGSBANK | SHILLING | 1818. Good. 16. .15

137 **Dijon**, In field. DIJON. *Rev.*, 5—CENTI. A line of silver extends across the planchet. Red, unc. 14. .40

138 **Dresden**, *Jetton*. HANNS BINER MVNCZMEISTER. 1561. Arms. *Rev.*, HIEF. LIBER. GOT. HIE VND DORT. Poor. 16. .12

139 **Dublin**. I PROMISE 20 SHILLINGS POUND STR. (Sterling). In field, Justice standing between two columns holding scales and sword; the date, 17–31, separated by her head. *Rev.*, CASH NOTES VALUE RECEIVED I MACULLA. In the field a large fleur-de-lis. Barely fair. 19. 2.00

140 **Durango,** *Ferd. VII.* F O VII. in a peculiar mon. crowned. *Rev.*, DURANGO | OCTAVO | DE | REAL. Beneath two branches joined in square knot. In ex 1816. Rude; the D in Durango is not in the planchet. Good. 15. 2.00

141 —— ¼ *Real.* OCTO. DE R de Do. 1828. In field, liberty cap radiated. *Rev.*, Indian boy with bow and arrow facing a cactus plant. Fair. 12. 1.25

142 *Octavo.* (¼ *Real*). REPUBLICA MEXICANA. The Mexican eagle upon cactus. *Rev.*, DEPARTMENTO DE DURANGO. In ex. 1847. In field, 8 DE REAL. Fair. 11. .40

143 —— ¼ *Reil.* DEPARTMENTO DE DURANGO as in preceding. *Rev.*, LIBERATAD EN EL ORDEN. In field, ¼. 1860. Fair. 17. .60

144 —— ¼ *Reil.* ESTADO DE DURANGO. Eagle as in No. 142. *Rev.*, INDEPENDENCIA Y LIBERTAD. In field ½ 1866. Beneath, two branches, crossed. Good. 17. .70

145 —— ¼ *Reil.* Similar to last. Lines indicating water beneath the cactus. *Rev.*, SUFRAGIO LIBRE 1872. In centre. ¼. Good. 17. 90

146 **Equador,** REPUBLICA DEL EQUADOR. Arms. In ex. 1872. *Rev.*, Dos | CENTAVOS between palm and laurel branches. Fair. 20. .70

147 **Eger,** Obsidional. Arms of the city; the shield divided into two parts, above, head and wings of an eagle; below, 8 lines crossed in diamond form. In ex. 3 K.(revzers). *Rev.*, EGER | 1743. 3 stars above, 1 below. Lead. Good. 13. 1.00

148 **Egypt,** *Abd-el-Aziz* 1277 (1861). 10 *Para.* Struck in the third year of the reign (1864). Red, unc. .18

149 —— TRAVAUX DU CANAL DE SUEZ. Ship under full sail r. within a circle of dots. In ex. EGYPTE. *Rev.*, BOREL LA VALLEY ET COMP¹ᴱ, 1865. Within a circle of dots. BON POUR 50 Centimes. Brass. Good. 13. .50

150 **Etruria,** *Maria Louisa* and *Chas. Louis*, 1803–7. M. ALOYSIA. R. R. C. LUD. R. ETR. &. Three fleur-de-lis upon an oval shield. *Rev.*, MEZZO | SOLDO. Fair. 13. .30

151 **Fano,** *Alex. VI.* 1492—1503. *Quattrino,* ALEXA VI PO MA, Papal Arms. *Rev.*, DE A SCVLO. A gateway with two towers ; between the towers a star. Good. 12. .25

152 **Fermo** REPVBLICA ROMANA Fasces and Lib. Cap. *Rev.*, DVE | BAIOCCHI | FERMO | 1798. Broad milled rim. Good. 22. .65

153 —— Legend as in preceding ANNO I (1798) within wreath of oak. *Rev.*, VN | BAIOCCO | FERMO Good. 19. .50

154 —— ANNO | PMO (1798) | DELLA REP. | ROMANA. *Rev.*, MEZZO | BAIOCCO | FERMO. Good. 17. 50

155 —— *Pius VI.* 2½ *Baicchi*, S. P. APOSTOLORUM PRINCEPS. Bust of St. Peter holding the keys of Heaven 1. *Rev.*, BAIOCCHI | DVE E MEZZO | FERMO. 1797. Good. 20. .40

156 —— Same. PTVS | PAPA VI | AN | XXIII. (23d year of reign). *Rev.*, MEZZO | BAIOCCO | FERMO | 1797. Good. 16. .40

157 **Ferrara,** *Alfonzo I.*, 1505–34. Quattrino. S. M'AVRELIVS PROTECT. Head of the saint r. *Rev.*, FERRARIAE surrounding a shield of two parts. Upper, *Sable,* lower, *plain.* Pierced with 3 minute holes. Fair. 10. .18

158 —— *Alfonzo II*, 1559–97. *Quattrino.* ALFONSVS II. DVX. In field, Eagle. *Rev.*, FERRARIAE. Upper portion of shield. *Sanguine.* Good. 10. .25

159 —— *Alex. VII.* *Mezzo Baiocco,* ALEXANDER VII. PONT. MAX. *Rev.*, FER | RARI | Æ | 1654. Obv. Fair. *Rev.*, Poor. 19. .25

160 —— *Clement X. Quattrino.* St. George killing the dragon. *Rev.,* FER | RARI | Æ | 1676. Fair. 12. .18

161 —— *Benedict XIV.* BENEDICT XIV. P. MA IV. Papal Arms. *Rev.,* 1 | BAIOCCO | FERRARA. In ex. date, 1744, divided by a cardinal's hat. Fair. 21. .30

162 —— Same. Year of reign being V. *Rev.,* MEZZO | BAIOCCO | FERRARA | 1745. Date divided as before. Fair. 17. .25

163 **Finland,** *Alex. II.* Letter A crowned. *Rec.,* 5 | PENNIA | 1872. Proof. 16. .25

164 **Flanders,** Philip II., 1555-98. *Demi Liard.* PHS. D. G. HISP. Z REX. COM. FLA. Bust l. In ex. a fleur-de-lis. m. m. of Bruges, *Rec.,* DOMINVS MIHI ADIVTOR. Arms crowned. Good. 14. .20

165 —— Same. *Demi Liard,* the m. m. (fleur-de-lis) separating the figures 9-1, (1591). *Rev.* as in preceding, but shield cut with Jerusalem cross. Fair. 13. .18

166 —— *Charles II, Liard.* CAROL II. D. G. HISP. ET INDIAR, REX. Crowned arms in form of cross. *Rev.,* ARCH. AVS. DVX. BVRG. C. FL. Crowned arms separating date. 16 93. Fair. 16, .15

167 **Florence,** *Republic,*1189-1315. *Quattrino.* S. JOHANNES B. St. John the Baptist, standing. *Rev.,* FLORENTIA. Fleur-de-lis. Fair. 8. .20

168 —— Similar (later period). S. JOAN NES B. *Rev.,* FLORENTIA. Fair. 11. .20

169 **France,** *Louis XIII.* DOVBLE TOVRNOIS, 1615. Bust r. Good. 13. .18

170 —— Same. DENIER TOVRNOIS, 1616. Fair. 10. .20

171 —— Same. DOVBLE TOVRNOIS, 1643. Head l. Good. 13. .20

172 **Frankfurt,** FURST PRIM. SCHEIDE MUNZE. A wheel in a crowned shield. *Rev.,* 1 | HELLER | 1810. Fair. 13. .15

173 **French Colonies,** *Louis Phillippe,* 1844. 10 *Centimes.* Head laureated r. Unc. 20. .30

174 **Fulda,** H(enricus) E(piscopus) F(uldensis) in crowned mon. *Rev.,* 1 | PFENNING | F. F. L. M. | 1769. Good. 13. .15

175 **Fuligno,** Pius VI. PIUS SEXTUS PON. M. A. XXI, (1795), Papal arms. *Rec.,* DVE | BAIOCCHI | DI | FVLIGNO. Broad milled rim. Good. 22. .60

176 —— Same. Year of Reign A XX, (1794). *Rev.,* VX | BAIOCCO | DI—FVLIGNIO. Fair. 20. .45

177 **Galicia,** (*Austrian Poland*). MONET AER EXERCIT CAES. REG. Imp. double headed eagle crowned, beneath which are six flags crossed, *Rev.,* 1 | GROSSVS | POL | 1794 Beneath, two branches crossed. Good. 14. .18

178 **Geldern,** Philip II, *Liard.* PHS. D. G. HIS. Z. REX. DVX. GEL. Crowned head to l. M. m. Small ornamented cross separating date, 15-87 Good. 18. .35

179 **Geneva,** Obsidional. Arms of the city. Eagle and key within the centre of the blazing sun. 8 tongues of flame shooting out from behind the shield; between the flames, 8 ornaments. *Rev.,* P X II | SOLS | POVR LES | SOLDATS DE | GENEVE | 1590. Unc. partly red. 19. 1.00

180 —— Same. But without the ornaments between the flames. *Rev.,* SIX | SOLS, etc. Good. 17. .75

181 —— Same. *Rev.,* P. VN | SOLS, etc. Fine. 13. .85

43

182 **Gerona,** Lvd. XIII, D. G R. F. E. C. Ba. Head l. *Rer.*,
Civitas Gervnda, 1642. Arms of the city in lozenge
shield. Fair. 15. .35
183 **Ghent,** XII. Ghent Myten. In field, lion rampant l.
between his feet, (15) 83. *Rer.*, Crowned arms. Nisi
Dvs. Frvstra. Fair. 17. .50
184  —— Royavme de Belgique, Gand, 1833. *Rer.*, Monnaie
Fictive. 5 Centimes. Good. 13. .40
185 **Gibralter,** Valve Two Quarts. In field, castle with 3
towers. In ex., a key. 1802. *Rer.*, View of the rock;
in the foreground the harbor, boats, etc. Payable at R.
Keeling's, Gibralter. Good. Obverse, fine. 19. .35
186 —— Same. Value One Quart. 1802. Good. 13. .25
187 —— Value Two Quartos. 1810. Castle as before. *Rer.*,
Lion holding key l. Payable at Robert Keeling &
Sons', Gibraltar. Fair. 18. .18
188 —— Same. Value One Quarto. Fine. 14. .20
189 —— Payable at Richard Catton's, Goldsmith. In field,
lion holding key. In ex., Gibraltar. 1813. *Rer.*,
"Agency for the Manufacture of Duddell's Patent Diamonds, Holborn," in Spanish. In field, a wreath, within
which is 2 Quartos ; above, a crown ; beneath, Londres.
Good. 18. .35
190 —— Same. *Rer.*, 1 Quarto within crowned wreath. Good.
13. .60
191 —— Payable at James Spittle's, Gibraltar. Lion and
key. *Rec.*, Vale dos Quartos. In field, a ruined
fortress. In ex., 1820. Fair. 18. .18
192 —— *Victoria*, 1842. *Two Quarts*. Bust. *Rer.*, Castle. Fine.
18. .35
193 —— Same, 1842. *One Quart*. Red. Unc. 14. .40
194 —— Same, 1842. *Half Quart*. Red. Unc. 12. .35
195 **Goa** (Portuguese India). *Joseph I.*, 15 *Reis*. Crowned arms
dividing the letters G. A. *her.*, 15 | 1769. Lead. Fair.
18. .40
196 **Gorz,** *Chas. VI.* Shield of two quarterings divided diagonally;
r., quarter, 2 bars; l., a lion rampant. *Rer.*, Soldi | 3 |
1734 | within a heavily ornamented shield. Good. 23. .65
197 —— Same. *Rer.*, Soldi | 2 | 1734. Good. 20. .50
198 —— Same. *Rec.*, Soldo | 1 | 1733. Good. 17. .35
199 —— Same. *Rer.*, Soldo | ½ | 1733. Fair. 15. .25
200 —— Same. 1 | Soldo | 1736. Good. 13. .25
201 —— *Francis I.* Similar arms. *Rer.*, 2 | Soldi | 1799 | S.
Good. 15. .15
202 —— Same. *Rer.*, 1 | Soldo | 1800 | H. Fair. 14. .15
203 **Gottingen.** Gothic G crowned. *Rer.*, 1621. III (*Pfgs.*)
Good. 10. .20
204 —— Letter R crowned, between 2 stars. *Rer.*, In field, III ;
surrounding, Pennige, 1621. Good. 10. .20
205 **Graubunden** (Swiss Canton). Arms, Kanton Graubunden.
In ex., 1820. *Rer.*, ½ | Schweiz | Batzen. Base. Good.
14. .15
206 **Greece,** *Capo d'Istria*, 1828. 10 *Lepta*, phœnix and cross
within circle. Good. 23. .35
207 —— Same, 1828. 5 *Lepta*. Good. 19. .20
208 —— Same, 1830. 10 *Lepta*. (Second coinage.) Good.
20. .25
209 —— Same, 1831. 10 *Lepta*. (Third coinage.) Good. 20. .30
210 —— Same. 1 *Lepton*. Fair. 11. .18

211 —— *George*. 1869. Bust l. *Rev.*, value and date. 10-5-2 & 1
*Lepta*. Red. Unc. 4 pcs. .70

212 **Groningen,** *Doit* Crowned arms supported by two lions; above
the crown the figures 1-6-9-0. *Rev.*, CIV | GRONIN | GA.
Fair. 14. .30

213 **Guanaxuato,** Liberty Cap radiated, 1828. *Rev.*, ESTADO
LIBRE DE GUANAJUATO, Seated female l. the head turned
toward her back. In ex. UNA CUARTILLA. Brass.
Poor. 18. .18

214 —— EST. LIBRE DE GUANAXUATO, 1856 In Field, Eagle on
Cactus. In ex. CUATILLA. *Rev.*, In field, an oval shield
containing two hands, one holding a miner's drill and the
other a hammer. Above, a lib. cap radiated, OMNIA
VINCIT LABOR. Beneath, laurel branches crossed. Brass.
Fair. 20. .75

215 —— Same. 1857. *Octavo.* Good. 16. 1.25

216 **Guastalla,** *Ferd. II., Soldo.* FERD. GON. MELF. P. G. COM.
Bust l. *Rev.*, INSIG. CVMVNIT. GVAS, 1621. In field, lion
running l. Fair. 12. .25

217 —— S. CATARINA PROTECTRIX. The saint standing. *Rev.*,
SESINO | DI GVAS | TALIA. Fair. 10. .25

218 **Gubbio.** *Innocent XII.*, 1691-1700. INNOC. XII. PONT. M.A.
10 (1701). Papal arms. *Rev.*, SANCT. PAVLIS AP., St.
Paul seated l. In ex. EVG(ubia). Fine. 15. .25

219 —— *Benedict XIII.* BENEDICTVS XIII., P. M. A. II. Papal
arms. *Rev.*, VN | BAIOCCO | GVBBIO | 1726. Fair. 26. .30

220 —— *Clement XII.* CLEMENS XII., P. M. A. I. Papal arms.
*Rev.*, VN | BAIOCCO | GVBBIO | 1731. Good. 23. .50

221 —— Same, 1731. Type and denomination of preceding.
Poor. .25

222 —— Same, with P. M. A, VIIII. *Rev.*, VN | BAIOCCO | GVBBIO
1739. Fair. 21. .25

223 —— *Benedict XIV.* BENEDICTVS XIV, P. M. AN. Papal
arms. *Rev.*, VN | BAIOCCO | GVBBIO | 1756. Fair. 23. .35

224 —— Same. BENE XIV., P. M. A. *Rev.*, MEZZO | BAIOCCO |
GVB. | 1754. Good. 18. .30

225 —— *Clement XIII.* CLEMENS XIII, P. M. Papal arms.
*Rev.*, VN | BAIOCCO | GVBBIO | 1759. Good. 23. .45

226 —— Same. CLEM. XIII., P. M. Papal arms. *Rev.*, MEZ. |
BAIOCCO | GVBBIO | 1759. Good. 17. .25

227 —— *Pius VI.*, 1775-99. PIVS SEXTVS PON. M. A. XX. (1795),
Papal Arms. *Rev.*, VN | BAIOCCO | GVBBIO. Good. 21. .35

228 —— Same, with A. XV (1790). *Rev.*, MEZZO | BAIOCCO | GVBBIO.
Good. 17. .20

229 —— Same. S. P, APOSTOLORUM, PRINCEPS. Bust of St.
Peter, holding the keys of Heaven, l. *Rev.*, BAIOCCHI |
DVE E MEZZO | DI | GVBBIO | 1796. Good, thick, but
slightly clipped. 19. .30

230 **Guinea,** *John III.* (of Portugal), 1521-27. PORTVGAL ET
ALGARB R. AFRIC. In field, Jo. III., above which is a
large crown. *Rev.*, Arms of Portugal. Fair. 18. 1.00

231 —— *Sebastian I.*, 1557-78. In field, SEBAS | TIA | NVS | 1.
Inscription surrounding, as in last. *Rev.*, as last. Fair.
18. 1.00

232 **Hainault,** *Philip II., Liard.* PHS. D.G. HISP. Z REX Co.
HAN. Crowned bust l. In ex, 15-85. *Rev.*, DOMINVS
MIHI ADIVTOR. Arms crowned. Poor. 17. .18

233 **Hamburg**, A castle with three towers. *Rev.*, THOR- | SPERRE
Good. 22. .25
[Note.—This is a token of the Turnpike Gate of the City.]

234 **Hanover**, *George V.*, G. R. in crowned mon. Beneath, a
small V. *Rev.*, 1 | PFENNIG | 1853. Red. Unc. 12. .15

235 **Hedwigsburg**. Arms in shield surmounted by a palm tree.
*Rev.*, 4 | QUARTIER | HEDWIGSBURG. Red. Unc. 15 .40

236 —— Same. 2 | QUARTIER | etc. Red. Unc. 13. .40
The two preceding pieces are brewery tokens.

237 **Hermosillo**. *Cuartilla.* HERMOSILLO A DE 1835 Lib.
Cap radiated. *Rev.*, EST D. SONORA. UNA CUART. An
arrow between two cornucopias. Fair. 14. .35

238 **Hesse-Cassel**. *Fred. II.* F (red) L (andgraf.) in mon. within
shield held by a lion. *Rev.*, 8 | HELLER | 1774. Good.
21. .30

239 —— **Hanau-Munzenburg**, *Wm. VIII.* W (m) L (and-
graf) in crowned mon. *Rev.* H | HELLER | HANAU |
SCHEIDE | MUNZE | 1745. Good. 14. .15

240 —— *Wm. IX.* HESS. HANAU MUNZENB. Crowned arms.
*Rev.*, 1 | KREU | ZER | 1773. Good. 17. .20

241 **Hildesheim**, shield of four quarterings, crowned. In 1st
and 3d a lion rampant l. *Rev.*, 1 | FLIT | TEN. Good.
9. .18

242 —— (Bishopric), *Fred. Wm.* Long inscription containing
the words HILD. PAD. and PYRM. Arms crowned. *Rev.*,
1 | PFENN | SCHEIDE | MUNZE | 1786. Good. 13. .15

243 **Honduras**, MONEDA PROVISIONAL DEL ESTADO DE HON-
DURAS upon a band surrounding a pyramid. *Rev.*, LIBRE
CRESCA FECUNDO. T (gucigalpa) 1862. A In field a
tree. 8 *Ps P(esos)*. Good. 25. .65

244 —— Same for 4 *Pesos*. Edge dented. Otherwise good. 20. .40

245 —— Same for 2 *Pesos*. Good. 16. .40

246 —— Same for 1 *Peso*. Good. 12. .35

247 **Hoxter**. An ornamented shield of two quarterings; upper,
10 lines crossed in diamond; lower, 3 pellets. *Rev.*,
blank. Good. 9. .30

248 **Hungary**, *Francis Rakoczky*. Crowned arms dividing date.
1705. *Rev.*. PRO LIBERATE. Virgin and child, dividing
P (atrona) H (ungary). In ex. XX (Poltura) in an ornamented square. Unc. Partly bright. 23. .60

249 —— Same. *Rev.*, X (Poltura). Good. 20. .30

250 —— Same. Beneath the date the letters C (ivitas) M (iskolcz).
X (Poltura). 20. .35

251 —— Same. POLTURA. A. 1705. Arms, dividing K (ör-
mocz) B (a'nya). m. in. of Kremnitz. *Rev.*, PATRONA
HUNGARIE. Virgin and child. Good. 15. .18

252 —— *Maria Theresa.* Bust r, with usual legend. *Rev.*, Virgin and child, radiated, dividing P.—H. 17—65. K.—
M. In ex. Poltura. Good. 20. .25

253 —— Same. 1766. *Greschel.* Crowned arms and legend.
*Rev.*, Virgin and child. PATRONA HUNGARIE. Good.
15. .18

254 —— Same. 1767. *Half Greschel.* Good. 13. .15

255 —— *Francis Joseph.* MAGYAR KIRALYI VALTO PENZ. Crowned
arms. *Rev.*, EGY | KRAJCZAR | 1848. Red. Unc. 11.
.25

256 —— Same. 1849. M. in. N. B. (*Nagy Banya*). Edge en-
grailed. Good. 17. .15

257 —— Same. Arms dividing 3 K(reuzers). *Rev.*, HAROM |
KRAJCZAR | 1849. Good. 21. .40

258 **Isle of Man,** Earl of Derby, *Penny.* SANS CHANGER. Eagle feeding a child lying in cradle upon a rock. (Arms of the Derbys.) In ex. 1700. *Rev.*, QVOCVNQVE GESSERIS STABIT. In field, the Trinacria. Original cast. Fair. 18. .45

259 —— Same. *Penny.* 1733. Type similar to preceding. *Rev.*, QUOCUNQUE IECERIS STABIT. Trinacria. *Cantonée* by I(ames) Derby) 1 (Penny). Good. 18. .40

260 —— Same. *Halfpenny.* Type same as last. *Rev.*, I. D. ½ between the legs of the Trinacria. Good. 16. .40

261 —— Duke of Athol. *Penny.* A. D. (Athol Duke) in crowned mon. In ex. 1758. *Rev.*, similar to last, but no letters between the legs of the Trinacria. Good. 18. .45

262 —— Same. *Halfpenny.* Good. 17. .45

263 —— George III. *Penny.* GEORGIVS III. DEI GRATIA. Bust r. In ex. 1786. *Rev.*, similar to last. Good. 21. .50

264 —— Same. *Halfpenny.* Good. 17. .40

265 —— Same. *Halfpenny.* GEORGIUS III. D G. REX. (Incused.) Bust r. In ex. 1798. *Rev.*, similar to preceding, but legend incused. Thick. Good. 17. .30

266 —— ISLE OF MAN, 1811. In field within a circle, BANK | PENNY. *Rev.*, similar to preceding. Fair. 21. .45

267 —— Same. *Rev.*, BANK | HALF | PENNY. Good. 17. .25

268 ——- PEEL CASTLE, ISLE OF MAN. View of the Harbor of Douglas. *Rev.*, DOUGLAS | TOKEN | ONE | PENNY | 1811. Fair. 20. .45

269 —— Same. *Rev.*, DOUGLAS | BANK | TOKEN | ONE | PENNY | 1811. Fair. 20. .50

270 —— MANKS' TOKEN, ONE PENNY, 1811. Trinacria. *Rev.*, PAYABLE AT THE OFFICE, DOUGLAS. Atlas bearing on the globe. (Issued by the Atlas Insurance Co.) Fair. 21. .40

271 —— Same. *Halfpenny.* Good. 18. .40

272 —— *George III.,* 1813. *Penny.* Type of 265. Good. 21. .50

273 —— Same. *Halfpenny.* Fair. 17. .15

274 —— *Penny.* GOD SAVE THE KING. Bust r. In ex. 1830. *Rev.*, FOR ' PUBLICK | ACCOMMODATION. Brass. Good. 22. .50

275 —— Same. In pure copper. Poor. .25

276 —— Same. *Halfpenny.* Good. 19. .30

277 —— Same. A copy of last. *Rev.*, is from the same die as Le Roux, 222 Canadian Token. Brass. Poor. 18. 1 00

278 —— PRO BONO PUBLICO, 1831 (Incused). In a sunken field. HALF | PENNY | TOKEN. *Rev.*, type of 265. Good. 18. .25

279 —— *Victoria,* 1839. *Penny.* Bust l. *Rev.*, Trinacria, etc. Fair. 21. .25

280 —— Same. 1839. *Halfpenny.* Fair. 18. .18

281 —— Same. 1839. *Farthing.* Good. 14. .20

282 **Ionian Isles,** *George III.,* 1819. *Two Oboli.* IONIKON KPATOE. Winged lion l. holding a bunch of 7 arrows. *Rev.*, BRITTANIA, Brit. seated l. Unc. 22. 90

283 —— Same. *Obolo.* Good. 18. .35

284 —— Same. ½ *Obolo.* Good. 14. .20

285 —— Same. ¼ *Obolo.* Fine. 10. .15

286 **Isny,** *Heller.* Crowned eagle, head l. Upon his breast an oval shield bearing a horseshoe. *Rev.*, blank. Fine. 8. .25

287 **Isole and Armata.** S. MARC VEN. Lion of St. Mark in ex. I. (*Soldo*). *Rev.*, ISOLE | ET | ARMATA. Fair. 15. .30

288 **Iviea.** (Eubusie). *Philip IV.* 1621-65. PHI. IIII. DEI G.
Rex MAN. Crowned head r. facing a large 6 (*Dineros*).
Re.r, VNIVER EBVSI DNS Castle. Poor (as all are). 14. .20

289 —— *Chas. II.* 12 *Dineros*. CAR. II. HISP. REX. ANNO,
1668. Crowned head r. Rer., MAGNI VNIVERITIS EBVSIA.
Crowned shield bearing 4 bars. Poor, but better than
usually found. 16. .65

290 **Jalisco.** ESTADO LIBRE DE JALISCO. Flag, bow and quiver.
In. ex. 1831. Rer., UN QUARTO, Lib. seated l. Good.
18. .50

291 —— Same. Rev., UN OCTAVO. Obverse fair. Rer., poor. 13,
.40

292 —— DEPARTMENTO DE JALISCO. 1859. Rer., UNA CUATILLA.
Counterstamped. 2. Fair. 20. .65

293 —— Same. Rer., UN OCTAVO. Fair. 18. .65

294 —— Same. Rer., MEDIO OCTAVO. Fair. 13. 1.00

295 **Japan.** ½—1—2 *Sen.* and 1 *Rin.* Red. Unc. 4 pcs. .50

296 **Julich** (During the strife for succession). 1592-1609. Mo.
Poss. PRIN. IVL. E. MON. Arms upon a cross dividing
date. 16-11. Rer., IVSTITIA THRONVM FIR. Arms
crowned. Fair. 16. .35

297 **Kempten** (Abbey). Double-headed eagle ; on the breast a
shield bearing the letter K . Rer., 1 | KREI | ZER. | 1622.
Fair. 11. .25

298 **Kingston** (Jamaica). THOMAS LUNDIE & CO., KINGSTON. In
Field. 1844. Rer. EARL OF ELGIN, JAMAICA. Brass.
Good. 15. .40

299 —— M. HOWARD FERRY GRASS. Coachman driving coach
and horses, r.; passenger within. Rer., KINGSTON,
JAMAICA. A groom holding a horse. Good. 19. .70

300 —— *Penny Token.* Arms supported by two Indians. Crest,
an alligator. Rer., PAYABLE IN KINGSTON, WILLIAM
SMITH (Incused). In sunken field, I. D. (inclosed in an
oval) JAMAICA | CURRENCY BY. Good. 19. .75

301 —— Same. PAYABLE, WILLIAM SMITH (Incused). In a
sunken field. IN KINGSTON BY. Rer., ONE-HALF PENNY
CURRENCY (Incused). In sunken field, JAMAICA. Good.
14. .75

302 **Laningen.** Crowned head l. Rer., the figure 4. Fair. 11. .30

303 —— Similar. Head much smaller. Rer., the letter L. in Ger-
man Script. Fair. 11. .40

304 **Leipzig.** A shield of two quarterings. Left, lion rampant,
right, 3 pales. Rer., Blank. 14. .45

305 **Lend,** 1726. Smelting-house token for 4 *Krzs.* H. F. L. in
mon. In ex. a bunch of grapes. Good. 13. .20

306 —— Same. 1720. 1 *Krzr.* F. and H. N. A. in mon. Rer.,
F. and H. G. in mon. Good. 11. .15

307 **Lerida,** PUG. ESAD. ELL. IDA. Three fleur-de-lis upon long
stems. Rer., three large fleur-de-lis as before. No legend.
Fair. 12. .30

308 —— Same. Fleur-de-lis upon obverse, within lozenge. Good.
13. .35

309 —— Same. PUG. ESA. DEL EDA. Fleur-de-lis within lozenge.
Rer., same as obverse. Fair. 12. .30

310 **Leon** (Nicaragua) Market *Token.* MERCADO | DE | LEON.
Rer., 2¼ | DIME. Poor. 14. .20

311 **Leyden,** *Half Stuber.* HEERE ONTBERMT. HOL. In field, a
crowned lion rampant l. dividing 7-4 (1574). Rer., ENDE
SALICHT LEYDEN. Shield with 2 keys crossed. Good.
16. .60

48

**312 Liberia.** Republic of Liberia (Incused) Head of Lib. l.
*Rev.*, Two Cents, 1847. In sunken field, a palm tree.
Good 22. .60
313 ——— Same. One Cent, 1862. Red. Unc. 18. .50
**314 Lindau,** *Heller.* A linden tree. *Rev.*, Blank. Good. 8. .25
**315 Lippe,** *Simon VI.*, 1563-1613. Lipp Lant Myntz. In field,
a rose. *Rev.*, III. (*Pfgs.*). Good. 13. .18
316 ——— Same. *Rev.*, II. (*Pfgs.*). Good. 12. .15
317 ——— Same. A rose. *Rev.*, ½ (*Pfg.*). Good. 10. 15
318 —— *Geo. Wm.*, 1858. 1 *Pfenning.* Rose in crowned shield.
Red. Unc. .18
319 ——— *Schaumberg, Geo. Wm.* Small rose within shield upon a
nettle leaf, which rests upon a crowned heart-shaped shield.
*Rev.*, 1 | Guter | Pfenning | 1824. Good. 13. .12
320 ——— Same. 1858. 1 *Pfg.* G. W. in crowned mon. Proof.
11. .25
**321 Lithuania,** *Shilling.* Joan Cas. Rex. Bust l. *Rev.*, Soli
Mag. Dvc. Lit., 1666. Chevalier mounted l. K. II.
L. L. in mon. Fair. 10 .18
**322 Los Angeles,** Maquinaria de los Angeles (machine shop
of Los Angeles). In field, M. Ynigo (in scrip), ¼. *Rev.*,
eagle on cactus. Republica Mexicana. In ex. Sonora.
Brass. 12. .50
**323 Lucca,** *Quattrino.* Otto Imperator. In field in form of a
cross, L. V. C. A. *Rev.*, S. Petrvs. St. Peter standing,
Good. 11. .20
324 ——— *Quattrino.* Lion holding shield l. In ex. 1691. *Rev.*,
Liberatas in crowned shield. Fair. 10. .18
325 —— *Bologuino,* Respvblica Lvcensis. L. V. C. A. as in No.
323. In ex. 1789. *Rev.*, Sanctvs Petrvs. St. Peter
standing. Good. 12. .25
326 ——— *Chas. Louis.* Carlo, L. D. B. I. D. S. Duca di Lucca.
In field, crowned fleur-de-lis. *Rev.*, | Soldo | 1826.
Good. 14. .25
327 ——— Same. Ducato di Lucca. In field, a crown. *Rev.*,
Mezzo | Soldo | 1826. Good. 11. .20
**328 Lucern,** Canton Luzern. 2 part shield r., plain l. azure.
*Rev.*, 1 | Rappen | 1846. Good. 11. .18
**329 Luxemburg,** *Maria Theresa.* Liard. Draped bust r. *Rev.*,
Ad | Usum | Ducatus | Luxem | 1757. M. m. for Brussels. Fine. 18. .40
330 —— Same. *Liard.* Lion before 5 bars within an oval crowned
shield. Long legend. *Rev.*, M. T. in crowned mon.
Clementia Justitia. Fair. 18. .25
331 —— Same. 1758. *Demi Liard.* Fair. 15. .20
332 ——*Leopold II.* Arms as in No. 330. Legend. *Rev.*, 1 | Sol
| 1700 | II. M. m. of Rochelle. Good. 20. .30
333 ——— Francis II. Lion in crowned shield diviving F. II. *Rev.*,
1 | Sol. | 1795. Cast from gun metal during the siege,
Nov. 1794, to July '95. Good. 20. .40
**334 Macereta,** A(nno) I, D(ella), L(ibertad) I(taliana) Fasces, etc.
*Rev.*, Qvatri | no | Macer. Good. 11. .40
**335 Majorca,** *Philip IV.*, 1621-65 *Dobler.* Philipvs Rex. Aragonvm, head l. *Rev.*, Majoricar Catolicvs. Cross.
Poor. 10. .15
336 ——— *Chas. II.*, 1665-1700. *Dobler.* Carolvs II. R. Avago.
Head r. *Rev.*, Majorica-rvin Cato. Cross. Fair. 9. .20
337 —— Same. *Dobler.* Head l. 1 behind. Fair. 10. .25

338 —— *Philip V. Treseta*, PHILIPVS. HIS. R. 1724. Bust, behind which is the figure 6. *Rer.*, MAJORIC CATOLIC. Crowned arms behind cross. Poor and pierced. 14. .25
339 —— *Louis I. Treseta*. LVDOVICVS HIS. R. Bust r. behind, 6. *Rer.*, MAJORIC CATOLES. Poor. 12. .12
340 **Malta,** *John de la Vallete*, 1557–68. *Grano*. F. Io. DE VALETTE M. Ho. H. shield of two quarterings. Right, a lion rampant. Left, a bird on a branch. *Rev.*, ORDO. HOS. HIERVSAL. Maltese cross. Very poor, but one of the *rarest* of the copper coins of this series. 10. .25
341 —— *Alof de Wignacourt*, 1601–22. *Grano*, F. ALOFIVS D WIGNA. Circular shield of four quarterings. 1st and 3d, a cross. 2d and 4th, three fleur-de-lis. *Rev* , HOSPITALI HIERVSALEM. In field, VT | COMMO | DIVS. Good, but slightly broken. 12. .40
342 —— Same. 3 *Piccoli*. WIGNACOV. *Rer.*, In field, a large 3. Poor. 11. .20
343 —— *Aloys Mendes de Vasconceilos*, 1622–23. *Grano*. F. L. MENDES DE VASCONCELLOS. M. shield of 4 quarterings. 1st and 3d a cross. 2d and 4th, 3 bars. *Rer.*, HOSPITALI HIERVSALEM. In field, VT | COMMO | DIVS. Fair. 12. .75
[Note.—Neither the great Stecki nor Rossi collections (replete with this series) contained a specimen of the coinage of this Grand Master whose reign was less than one year. Neumann says "*sekr selten*."]
344 —— *John Paul Larcaris de Castellar*, 1636–57. 4 *Tari*. JOANNES PAVLVS LASCARIS, M. M. H. H. Crowned arms. *Rer.*, NON. AES. SED. FIDES. In field, 1641 T. 4. Counterstamped with the head of John the Baptist, fleur-de-lis, double headed eagle and star, each crowned. Fair. 21. 1.25
345 —— Same. 4 *Tari*. Type of last, counterstamped with star, diamond, crescent, fleur-de-lis, eagle, and pascal lamb. Fair. 23. 1.25
346 —— Same. Similar design. 2 *Tari*, counterstamped with crowned diamond, star and eagle. The original type nearly obliterated. This denomination is much *rarer* than the preceding. 17. .60
347 —— Same. Another piece of 2 *Tari*, in about the same condition, counterstamped with a crescent diamond, fleur-de-lis, and head of John the Baptist. 17. .75
348 —— Same. *Taro*. F. Jo. PAVLVS LASCARIS. M. H. H. Double-headed eagle. *Rer.*, SVB HOC SIGNO MILITAMVS. Maltese cross with 1—6—3—7 in the angles. Poor. 12. .25
349 —— *Raimond Perellos de Roccaful*. TARO. RECTAM FACIT. SEMITAN. Pascal lamb, 1. *Rer.*, IN HOC SIGNO MILITANVS. Date as in last, 1-7-1-8. Fair. 12. .40
350 —— *Anton Manuel de Vilhena*. 10 GRANI. F. D. AN MANO EL DE VILHENA. A hand holding a sword within a crowned shield. *Rer.*, NON AES SED FIDES. In field, hands clasped above. 1734. Beneath, X (Grani). Fair. 16. .40
351 —— *Raimund Despuig*, 1736–41. *Taro.* F. D. RAIMV DESPVIG. M. M. H. H. A pyramid surmounted by a cross. *Rer.*, type of last. 1-7-3-9. Fair. 12. .25
352 —— *Emanuel Pinto de Fouseca*. 20 GRANI. CONCVTIATIS NEMINEM. Head of John the Baptist upon the charger. *Rer.*, type of 350. 1742. XX. Good. 17. .65
353 —— Same. 20 *Grani*. Type of last. CON. CVTIATIS NEMINEM. The head l. 1762 XX. Fair. 17. .45
354 —— Same. *Grano*. F. EMMANVEL PINTO. M. M. H. H. 5 crescents. *Rer.*, type of 349. 1-7-7-5. Good. 10. .30

355 —— *Emmanuel de Rohan.* Taro. F.. Emmanvel de Rohan. M. M. Arms of four quarterings in a crowned
shield, supporters, the legs and wings of an eagle. 1st and
4th a Cross, 2d and 3d, 9 Diamonds. T (aro) I, divided by
the crown. *Rer.*, Non Aes Sed Fides. Head of
John the Baptist on the charger. In ex. 1786. Good.
16. .50

356 —— Same. 10 *Grani.* Design similar to last. Shield con
tains 9 diamonds (the family arms). *Rer.*, type of No.
350. 1786 X. Fair. 14. .40

357 —— Same. 5 *Grani.* Similar design to last. *Rec.*, as last.
1790 V. Good. 12. .40

358 —— Same. *Grano*, legend as last, the family arms occupy-
ing the entire field. *Rec.*, Non Aes. Sed Fides 1776.
In Field G. 1. Good. 10. .35

359 —— Same. *Grano.* Same as last, but on *Rer.* has date 1785
under the denomination. G.1. Fair. 10. .25

360 —— *George IV.*, 1827. ⅓ *Farthing.* Type of his 2d coinage
for England. Fine. 12. .30

361 —— *Victoria.* Bust l. *Rer.*, One-Third | Farthing | 1866.
Red, unc. 10. .40

362 **Malwah,** *Hassan, Schah,* 1500–12. *Piassa.* Gheras Schah
Sultan. *Rec.*, Sultan Son of Sultans 912 (1506) in
native characters. Fair. 12x12. .35

363 —— *Mahmud II.*, 1512–44. *Pai.* Similar to last. Fair.
9x9. .25

364 **Mantua,** *Francis II.*, 1484–1519. *Quattrino*, Franciscvs.
Mr. Mantve IIII. Bust l. *Rer.*, D. Probasti me. et,
Cogno Mi. Crucible amid flames. Good. 11. .25

365 —— Same. *Quattrino.* Franc Mar. Mant. IIII. Dog
seated l. *Rec.*, Xpi Ihes. Sangvin. In field, a chalis.
Fair. 11. .30

366 —— Same. *Quattrino*, Franc Mant. Mar. IIII. Bust l.
with cap. *Rec.*, similar to last. Fair. 11. .25

367 —— Same. *Quattrino* Franci Mav. Man. IIII. Bust l.
with hat. *Rer.*, similar to last. Fair. 11. .25

368 —— Same. *Quattrino.* Vigilivs Maro. Bust l. *Rer.*,
E. (piscorom) P. (rinceps) O (minum). Beneath a tulip.
Good. 11. .18

369 —— *Frederick II.*, 1519–40. *Quattrino.* Fe II. M. Mantvae
IIII. Youthful head l. *Rer.*, Fides. A pyramid
with grape vine growing over it. Fair. 11. .25

370 —— Same. *Quattrino.* Type similar to last, but the face is
bearded. *Rec.*, OAΓ | ΛΗΙΣ. Fair. 11. .18

371 —— Same. *Quattrino.* Fed. Dvx M. T E (in mon.) Mav.
Mo. Te. Bearded head l. *Rer.*, similar to last. Good.
11. .20

372 —— *William*, 1550–87. *Quattrino.* Gvl. Dvx. Man. III.
E. Mav. M. F. Child's head, l. *Rer.*, Chalis, etc., as
in 366. Fair. 10. .20

373 —— *Vincent I.*, 1587–1612. *Quattrino.* Vin D. G. Dvx Mant.
IIII. In field within a crescent. Sic. *Rer.*, et Montio
Ferrat. Two letters C *dos à dos.* Fair. 10. .20

374 —— *Vincent II.*, 1626–27. *Soldo.* Vin | II D. G. | Dvx | Man
VII et | etc. *Rer.*, Ship under full sail r. Above the
main-mast a star. Fair. 13. .40

375 —— *Chas. I.*, 1627–37. *Soldo.* Accensvs Sangvine In
Hostes. An Elephant l. *Rer.*, Nihil Isto Triste
Recept. In field, 2 challees, showing the sacred wafers
within. Good. 15 .40

376 ——— Same. *Sesino.* VIRGILIVS MAR. MAN. Head laureated l. *Rer.*, CAROL | 1 D. G. DVX | MANTVÆ | MON FER ¡ TE C. Fair. 13. .25

377 ——— *Chas. II. Sesino.* CAR II., D. G. DVX MANT. Bust l. *Rev.*, ET MONTIS FERATI, etc. 1661. Blazing sun. Fair. 12 .25

378 ——— Same. *Quattrino.* CAROLOS II , D. G. DVX. Head l. *Rer.*, MAN | TV | A. Fair. 10. .30

379 ——— *Ferd. Chas* , 1665-1708, *Soldo.* FERD. CAR. D. G. DVX MAN. X. In field, a pyramid and a crown. between which is the word FIDES. *Rev.*, ET. MONTIS FERRATI, VIII. Jerusalem cross, *Cantonée* with 4 crosslets. Fair. 11x12. Thick. .30.

380 ——— Same. *Sesino.* FER. | CAR. | D. G. D. *Rec.*, Man | E. T. (in mon.) M. F. | C. V. G. Good. 13. .20

381 ——— Same. F. C. In double mon. Crowned. *Rer.*, SESINO | DI | MAN. | TOVA | 1706. Fair. 12. .25

382 ——— *Chas. VI.* CAR. IMP. DVX MAN. Blazing sun. In ex. 1731. *Rev.*, SOLDO | DI MAN | TOVA. Fair. 14. .20

383 ——— Same. A cross. In ex. 1733. *Rer.*, SESINO | DI MAN | TOVA. Good. 12. .20

384 ——— Obsidional. ASSEDIO DI MANTOVA. Fasces. In ex. A (nno) 7 R(epublicana). · *Rev.*, UN | SOLDO | DI | MILAN. Good. 17. .35

385 **Mansfield,** Shield of 4 quarterings in form of a heart. 1st and 3d two bars; 2d and 4th an eagle. Above, III. *Rec.*, 3 (*Pfgs.*) in similar shield. Fair. 11. 40

386 ——— Shield quartered with 2 lions, eagle, and 2 leaves joined by a stem. At either side and above, a small circle in form of letter O. *Rev.*, Imperial. apple. 3 (Pfgs.) above, 16-21. Fair. 10. .35

387 **Maranhao,** *Peter I.* IN HOC SIGNO VINCES. Arms of Brazil crowned. *Rev.* PETRUS I. D. G. CONST. IMP. ET PERF. BRAS. DEF. In field within a wreath. 37½. (*Reis*) M. Good. 19. 2.00
[Note.—This is the only specimen I have ever met with.]

388 **Mayence,** R(hein) T(hor). A wheel. *Rev.*, 1 | KREU (zer). Oval. 13x16. Good. .30

389 ——— B(rücken) Z(oll). Wheel II. KR. *Rev.*, same. Good. 15. .20

390 ——— C(assler) S(eite) 1 KR. | B.(rucken) Z.(oll) *Rev.*, same. Fair. 15. .25
[Note.—The three lots preceding are Bridge Tokens.]

391 **Mecklenburg-Schwerin,** FRIED. FRANZ II., 1872, 5-2-1. *Pfg.* Red. Unc. 3 pcs. .35

392 **Merida,** MERIDA DE YUCATAN. In Field. PART. | D. LA So-CIED. In ex., 1856. *Rev.*, 2 GRANO | DE PESO | FUERTE Lead. Fair 17. 1.25

393 **Mexico,** *Charles I.* and his Mother *Johanna*, 1506-55 KARO-LVS ET JOHANNA REGES. In field, letter K crowned, to right a lion, left a castle, below the figure 4; beneath the castle the m. m. Mo. *Rer.*, HISPANIARVM ET INDI-ARVM. I. Crowned, to right a lion, left a castle, below the figure 4. Barely fair. 17. 3.50

394 ——— *Ferd. VII.*, 1808-21. *Double Quartilla.* Arms of Castile and Leon. In the centre 3 lilies. In ex. a pomegranate. *Rev.*, 2 4. A rude necessity piece. Good. 14. .75

395 ——— Same. *Quartilla.* Lion l. *Rev.*, ½. Good. 11. .45

396 ——— Same. *Double Quartilla.* FERDIN. VII. D. G. HISP. REX. 1816. In field F. VII. in mon. dividing —Mo. *Rer.*, arms of Castile and Leon. Good. 18. .40

397 —— Same. *Quartilla.* Type of last, 1814. Mo.—¼. Fair. 13. .25
398 —— Same. *Octavo*, 1815. Mo—⅛. Poor. 11. .15
399 —— *Republic.* OCTAVO. REPUBLICA MEXICANA. Eagle on cactus. *Rev.*, ¼. Mo. A., 1829. Fair. 18. .60
400 —— Same. *Quartilla.* Type and *size* of preceding. *Rev.*, ¼. Nearly fine. .35
401 —— Same. 1833. *Octavo. Rev.*, ¼. Fair. 18. .30
402 —— Same. Copy of 399. *Rev.*, UNA CUARTILLA. Liberty cap within a circle of radiated clouds. In ex. 1836. Proof. 18. 1.50
403 —— Same REPUBLICA MEXICANA. Head of Lib. r. In ex. 1838. *Rev.*, 1 | CUARTILLA | GA (Guanaxuato). Brass. Unc. 19. 1.60
404 —— Same. Obverse as last. *Rev.*, UNA | CUATILLA | ZS. (Zacatecas.) Brass. Unc. 19. 1.60
405 —— Same. LIBERTAD. Liberty seated r. In ex. L. ROVIRA F. (*small*). *Rev.*, OCTAVO | DE REAL | 1841. Edge inscribed REPUBLICA MEXICANA. Fair. 18. .35
406 —— Same. 1842. Same as last. Fair. .35
407 —— Same. LIBERTAD Y REFORMA. Lib. seated r. In ex. FAREDES. (*small*.) *Rev.*, UN | CENTAVO | 1863 within heavy wreath. In ex. Mo. Fine. 1.00
408 —— *Maximillian*, IMPERIO MEXICANA. Eagle on cactus. *Rev.*, 1 | CENTAVO | 1864 | M. Poor. 16. .40
409 —— Republic. REPUBLICA MEXICANA. Eagle on cactus. *Rev.*, UN | CENTAVO | 1876 | CN (Culiacan). Fair. 16. .15
410 —— Same, 1877. m. m. PI. (Potosi). Fair. .80
411 —— Same, 1879. m. m. DO. (Durango). Fair. .30
412 —— Same, 1880. m. m. GO. (Guanaxuato). Fair. .30
413 —— Same, 1881. m. m. GA. (Guadalaxara). Fair. .30
414 —— Same, 1881. m. m. HO. (Hermiosillo). Fair. .30
415 —— Same, 1881. m. m. MO. (Mexico). Fair. .20
416 —— Same, 1881. m. m. ZS. (Zacatecas). Fair. .30

417 **Milan.** *Francis II*, 1522–35. *Trillina.* FRANC SECVNDVS. In field, 3 pineapples. *Rev.*, MEDIOLANI DVX. A ring crowned, ornamented with leaves. Fair. 10. .25
418 —— Same. *Trillina.* Legends as before. Cross. *Rev.*, F. II., crowned. Good. 11. .25
419 —— *Philip III*, 1598–1621. *Trillina.* PHILIP III., REX. HISP. Head r. *Rev.*, MEDIOLAN DVX. ET C. cross. Eagles and serpents in the angles. Good. 10. .25
420 —— Same. *Philip IV.* 1621–'65, *Sesino.* PHILIPP IIII. REX. H. Bust r. *Rev.*, as last, serpent crowned. Fair. 12. .25
421 —— *Chas. VI. Quattrino*, CAROLVS VI, IMP. ET, H. R. Bust r. In ex. 1736. *Rev.*, MLNI | DVX. ; above, a crown. Fair. 8x10. .18
422 —— *Maria Theresa*. M. THERESA, D. G. R. I. (etc.) D. MED. Bust r. *Rev.*, UN | SOLDO | 1777. Fine. 15. .20
423 —— Same. Legend similar to last. Crowned arms. *Rev.*, MEZZO | SOLDO | 1777. Good. 13. .12
424 —— Same. Type of last. *Rev.*, UN ∫ QUATTRINO | 1777. Fine. 11. .18
425 **Minorca,** *Alfonso V.* 1416–58. ALFONSUS REX. Bust l. *Rev.*, MINORICKARUM, arms. Fair. 11. .60
426 **Mirandola,** 1515-33. *Quattrino*, I(ohn), F(rancisco), P.(ico) | MIRAN | DOM | C. C. *Rec.*, Blank. Fair. 9. .18
427 —— 1637-91. *Soldo.* ALEX. II., DVX. MIRAND. Crowned arms. *Rev.*, MI | RANDV | LÆ. Fair. 13. .30
428 **Modena** (Mutina) *Sesino.* Eagle crowned. *Rev.*, MVT ∫ SESIN. Fair. 11. .20

429 —— *Sesino*, Fleur-de-lis. *Rer.*, Mvt | sesin. Fair. 10. .25
430 —— *Cæsar*. 1597-1628. *Quattrino*, Cæsar Dvx. Head l.
     *Rer.*, Mvtinae Reg. Eagle. Good. 11. .25
431 —— *Alfonso IV*. 1658-62. Alph. IV. M. R. E. C. D. IX.
     In ex. E. T. Bust r. *Rev.*, Mvtin | Sesin. Good.
     10. .25
432 —— *Rainold I.* 1694-1737. ½ *Bolignino*. Rayn I. Mvt. R.
     Ec. Dvx. XI. *Rev.*, Mezzo | Bo | Logni. Base.
     Fair. 12. .25
433 —— Same. *Sesino*. Rayn I. Mvt Reg. Dvx. Bust r.
     *Rer.*, Mvt | Sesin. Fair. 12. .25
434 —— *Hercules III.* Eagle in draped shield dividing date
     17-83. *Rer.*, Vn | Bologni | no. Fair. 14. .25
435 **Montferrat.** *Wm II.* 1493-1518. *Quattrino.* Montis
     Ferra. In field, G. M., crowned. *Rer.*, S. Evaxivs
     Cvstos. A blazing cross, dividing S.(anetus) V.(asius).
     Good. 10. .25
436 **Mozambique.** 40 *Reis.* Maria II. D. G. Portug et Alg.
     Regina. *Rev.*, Pecunia totem circumvit Orbem.
     40 | 1840. Unc. 20. .70
437 —— Same. 1840. 20 *Reis.* Type of last. Fine. 16. .50
438 **Namur.** Phil. V. D. G. Hispania et India Rex. Bust r.
     *Rev.* Dux Burgund Braban Z. 2——L(iards) and date
     17-09 divided by crowned arms. m. m., a lion. Good, 18.
     .45
439 —— Same. 1710. *Liard.* Legend similar to last. 3 shields
     and crown in form of a cross. m. m., a lion. *Rer.*,
     similar to last. Good. 17. .20
440 —— *Maria Theresa.* Demi Liard. Bust r. Necklace of
     Beads. M. T(etc) D. Burg. *Rer.*, Ad | Usum | Belgii
     | Austr. | 1749. m. m. beneath date. Good. 15. .20
441 **Naples.** *James II.* 1285-95. *Torneso.* Jacobvs Dei Gra-
     tia. Rex. Small star with 3 curved arms. *Rer.*, Crvx
     Pellit oa crii. Fair. 13. .25
442 —— *Henry of Lorraine.* (Duke of Guise). 3 *Tornesi.* Hen
     de Lor. Dvx. Rei. Crowned shield inscribed
     S(enatus) P(opulis) Q(ue) N(apoli). *Rev.*, Pax et
     Vbertas. 1648. Three heads of wheat and branch
     crossed. Good. 18. .60
443 —— Same. 3 *Tornesi.* Similar to last. *Rer.*, Hinc Liber-
     tas. Basket containing six heads of wheat. In ex.
     1648. Rude. Oval. 14x18. Fair. .45
444 —— Same. 1648. Type of preceding. Reip. N. *Rer.*,
     Similar to last. Fair. 16. .50
445 **Navarre.** *Henry II.* 1516-55. Liard. Henri Dei G.
     Rex. Navar. D. B. In field, H crowned. *Rev.*, Gra.
     Dei. Svm. id Qvod. Svm. Cross. Good. 11. .60
446 —— *Phil II.* 1556-98. *Dinero.* Sit nomen Dom. In
     field, N. *Rec.*, Plvs Vltr. Pillars of Hercules crowned.
     Enclosing m. m. P(ampaluna). Fair. 11. .50
447 —— *Phil. III. Cuarto* P. II. S. D. G. R. N. A. In field, F.
     I. | 4. Crowned. *Rer.*, I. N. S. A. N. 1. 6 X. (1610).
     Arms of Navarre, crowned. Fair. 14. .35
448 —— Same. *Cuarto.* Design similar to last, with date. 1612.
     Fair. 14. .35
449 —— *Phil. IV.* Cuarto. Phs. D. G. Rex, Navar. In field
     F. I. | 4. Crowned. *Rer.*, Insig. Navar A. 1622.
     Crowned arms dividing m. m. P.—A. (Pampaluna). Fair.
     12. .40

450 —— *Ferd. III.* (VII. of Spain). FERDIN III. D. G. NAVARRÆ
REX. Laureated head r. dividing 3—M (aravedis). In ex.
1820. *Rer.*, CHRISTIANA RELIGIO. Arms upon a crowned
Maltese cross. m. m. P. P. (Pampaluna). Good. 16. .35
451 —— Same. 1820. Type of last. 1—M (aravedi). Fair. 12.
.35
452 —— Same. 1826. Type of preceding, but head not laureated.
3—M (aravedis). Good. 16. 40
453 —— Same. 1826. As last. 1—M (aravedi). Good. 11. .30
454 —— Same. FERDINANDUS III. D. G. Bust r. 3—M (aravedis). In ex. an ornament. *Rer.*, NAVARRÆ REX.
Crowned arms dividing m. m. P.— P. In ex. 1830.
Fair. 17. .35
455 —— Same. 1833. Type of last. 1—M (aravedi). Fine.
11. .40
456 —— *Isabel II.* ISABEL 2A. POR LA G. DE DIOS Y LA CONST.
Bust. r. In ex. 1837. *Rec.*, REYNA DE LAS ESPAÑAS.
Arms of Castille and Leon. In ex. 8 (P P) M. Brass.
Original east, Oct. 1837. (Neumann, 14,564). Fair. 19.
.75
[Note.—This is the only specimen of this piece I have ever met with.]
457 **Neuchatel,** *Alexander.* ALEXAN. PR. & DUC DE NEUCH.
Crowned arms. *Rev.*, PRINCEPS ANT. DE NEUCHATL. In
field, 1 | GREUT. In ex. 1807. Good. 12. .25
458 **New Biscay,** (State of Durango, Mexico.) *Octavo.* Crowned
arms. D—¼. *Rer.*, DE LA | PROVINCIA | DE NUEVA |
VIZCAYA | 1822. Fair. 12. 1.00
459 **Nicaragua,** *Quartilla.* A lion rampant l. *Rec.*, N. R. (in
mon.) ¼. Good. 8. .65
460 **Nuremburg.** Shield of two parts; r. 3 chevrons, l. half of
an eagle ; above, the letter N. *Rev.*, 1 | KREUTZ | ER |
1622. Good. 12. .20
461 **Oruro** (Bolivia) GOLDEN BALL HOTEL.—BOLA DE ORO. A
Ball within a shield. *Rer.*, MEDIO | REAL. Fine. 13 .25
462 **Palma Nova.** Obsidional MONTA D. ASSED PALMA. In
field, a crown. 1814. *Rer.*, NAPOLEONE IMPE E RE.
In field, CENT (esimos) 50. Fair. 18. .70
463 **Papal States.** GREGORIVS XVI. PONT. MAX. A. XI. Arms.
*Rer.*, BAIOCCO | 1841. Good. 19. .20
464 —— Same. *Rer.*, MEZZO | BAIOCCO | 1841. Fine. 15. .18
465 —— Same. XIII Year of Succession. *Rer.*, QVATTRINO |
1843. Good 12. .15
466 —— *Pius IX,* PIO—NONO. Arms. *Rer.*, PONT. MAX. In
field, 2 | BAIOCCHI. In ex. 1848. To the right of date a
small temple, to left the letter G. Crowned. m. m. of
GAIETA. Brass. Une. 18. .1.50
467 —— Same. 2d coinage. PIVS IX. PON. MAX. ANN. IV.
Arms. *Rer.*, BAIOCCO | 1849. Good. 19. .15
468 —— Same. III Year. *Rev.*, MEZZO | BAIOCCO | 1848 | R
Fine. 15. .15
469 —— Same. 3d Coinage. Similar to last. *Rev.*, 5 | BAIOCCHI
| 1850 | R. Good. 25. .30
470 —— Same. *Rev.*, 2 | BAIOCCHI | 1851 | R. Good. 22. .20
471 —— Same. *Rer.*, 1 | BAIOCCO | 1850 | R. Good. 19. .15
472 —— Same. *Rev* , ½ | BAIOCCO | 1850 | R. Good. 15. .15
473 —— Same. 4th Coinage. PIVS IX. PONT. MAX. ANN.
XXIII. Bust l. In ex. 1868. *Rev.*, STATO PONTIFICIO.
CENTESIMI. In field, 4 | SOLDI | R. Fine. 23. .35
474 —— Same. 1867. 2 | SOLDI | R. Fine. 21. .25
475 —— Same. 1867. 1 | SOLDO | R. Good. 17. .18
476 —— Same. 1866. ½ | SOLDO | R. Good. 15. .18
477 —— Same. 1866. 1 | Centesimo. Good. 10. .25

478 **Paraguay,** REPUBLICA DEL PARAGUAY. In field, $\frac{1}{12}$ (Real.)
In ex. 1845. *Rev.* Lion seated before a pole support-
ing a radiated liberty cap. Good. 15. .40
479 —— REPUBLICA DEL PARAGUAY. Radiated star between
palm and laurel branches. *Rev.*, CENTESIMOS | 4. In
ex. 1870. This piece, although the type of the regular
coinage of the year, does not bear the name of the die-
cutter, as does that following, as well as differing in other
respects. It is on a rough planchet, and is unquestion-
ably of native workmanship. Good. 23. 1.00
480 —— Same. 1870. Design as last. The die-cutter's name,
SHAW, at right of date. *Rev.*, CENTESIMOS | 2. Good.
18. .35
481 **Parma,** *Ranutius II.* 1646—94. RANVT. FAR. PAR. ET.
PLA. DVX VI. Crowned Arms. *Rev.*, SESINO | DI |
PARMA. Fair. 14. .25
482 —— Same. *Denaro.* RAN. F. DVX VI. Crowned Arms.
*Rev.* S. ANT. M. PRO. PL. St. Antonio mounted l.
Good. 10. .20
483 **Parthenopean Republic.** (Naples), Jan'y to July, 1799.
NEPOLITANA REPUBLICA. Fasces and lib. cap. *Rev.*,
ANNO SETTIMO DELLA LIBERTA. In field, TOR | NESI |
SEI | ZN. Good. 22. .65
484 —— Same. As last, but without Z. N. Good. 22. .75
485 —— *Rev.*, Type of last. *Rev.*, TORNE | SI | QUAT | TRO.
Fair. 18. .40
486 **Piedmont,** Republic, 1798—1802. LIBERTA EGUAGLIANZA.
Triangle and plumb-line surmounted by lib. cap.; be-
neath. A. 9 (1802). *Rev.*, NAZIONE PIEDMONTESE. In
field, SOLDI | *due* (in script). Good. 18. .40
487 **Pergola,** (under Roman Republic). VN | BAIOCCO | PERGOLA
1798. *Rev.*, VN | BAIOCCO | PERGO | LA. In ex. m. m.
P. Fair. 21. .60
488 **Peru.** Llama, mountains, blazing sun, lib. cap, etc.
*Rev.*, REPUBLICA PERUANA. M. In field, QUARTO | DE
PESO. In ex. 1823. Good. 17. .60
489 —— Same. 1823. Type of last. *Rev.*, OCTAVO | DE PESO.
Good. 14. .50
490 **Perugia,** *Quattrino,* AVGVSTA PERUSIA. Crowned Lion rampant, l. *Rev.*, SANTVS ERCVLANVS. In field, P. Fair.
10. .20
491 —— *Quattrino,* DE PERUSIA. In field, P. *Rev.*, S.
ERCVLANVS. Cross. Fair. 10. .25
492 —— *Pius VI.* 5 BAIOCCHI, SANCTA DEI GENITRIX. Bust of
the Virgin, with Nimbus. *Rev.*, PIVS SEXTVS ANNO
XXIII, 1797. In field, BAIOC | CINQVE | PERVGIA.
Good. 20. .40
493 **Pesaro,** *John Sforza.* 1489-1500. *Soldo.* JOANNES SFORTIA
PISAVRI DOMI. Bust r. *Rev.*, PV | BLICÆ | COMMO |
DITA | TI. Good. 13. .40
494 —— *Guido Ubaldus II.,* 1538-94, *Quattrino.* G. V. | 11.
Crowned in field. *Rev.*, A crown from beneath which
flames are issuing. Fair. 11. .18
495 **Pesth,** *Chas. VI.,* 1711-40. Austrian double-eagle crowned.
C VI, upon a band across the breast. *Rev.*, 2 (Kreuzers).
Good. 15. .25
496 —— Same. 1 *Kreuzer.* Fair. 12. .20
[Note.—Both this and the preceding are Tokens of the Military Hospital.]
497 —— Gateway of Egyptian Architecture, with long perspective
view of a tunnel. Above tree-tops are visible. *Rev.*,
Incused. Good. 17. (Token for Tunnel connecting
Buda-Pesth.) .20

498 —— A bridge with four towers. Boatman beneath. *Rev.*, Incused, Good. 17x17. (Token for Chain Bridge connecting Buda-Pesth.) .20

499 **Petau,** PURG. FRIDTS BEREITUNG ZU PETAU, 1769. Arms a large cross in a shield Above, F.(raucis) W.(urth) (Die-sinker in Vienna). Below, AUGUSTI | 28. *Rev.*, St. George and the Dragon. Good. 14. 30

500 **Philippine Islands,** *Ferd. VII.* FERN VII. P. L. G. D. Y. LA CONST. R. D LAS E. Bust r. *Rev.*, VTRAP VLTRA PROTEG MAN C. Arms of Spain crowned, dividing 1-Q(uarto). In ex. 1823. Fair. 14. .60

501 —— Same. *Quarto.* FERD. VII. D. G. HISP. ET. IND. R. MA. 1-Q. *Rev.*, VERT. PROTEGO. Lion with crown and sceptre resting his right paw upon two globes, r. In ex. F. 1834. MA. Good. 14. .35
[Note.—It is probable that the Islanders had not learned of the death of the king and the accession of Isabel II.]

502 —— *Isabel II.* YSAB. II., D.G. HISP. ET IND. R. M. R. Crowned Arms of Spain, dividing 4-Q(uartos). *Rev.*, UTRAP. UIRT PROTEGO. Lion as before. In ex. F. 1835, MA. Good. Thick. 21. .75

503 —— Same. 1835. Type of last. 2-Q(uartos). Fair 17. .35
[Note.—The last four lots were minted at Manilla, the m. m. of which city they bear. They are the best specimens I have met with, and may fairly be termed *rare.* Of 500 and 502 I have seen no duplicates.]

504 **Pondicherry,** Three fleur-de-lis. *Rev.*, 1769. Good. Thick. 9. .30

505 **Poland,** *John Casimir. Shilling,* IOAN CAS. REX. Bust r. *Rev.*, SOLI REGNI POL. 1661. Eagle. Fair. 10. .15

506 —— *Augustus III.* AUGUSTUS III., REX. POL. Bust r. *Rev.*, E. L.(ector) SAX(ony), 1755. In ex., 3 (Shillings). Crowned arms. Good. 13. .25

507 —— *Stanislaus Augustus.* S.(tanislaus) A.(gustus) R. (ex.), in mon. crowned, dividing date 17–90. *Rev.*, 1 GROSSUS REG. POL. M. D. L. Crowned arms. In ex. E(phraim) B(renn), Mint-Master in Warsaw. 1774–92. Good. 13 .18

508 —— Same, 1766. *Rev.*, ¼ | GROSSUS | REG. | POL. | G(artenburg Mint-master). Good. 11. .15

509 **Portugal,** *John III.,* 15 21–27. 10 *Reis.* IOANES III. D. G. POR. ET ALGARBIORVM. Crowned arms. *Rev.*, REX QVINTVS DECIMVS. In field, large X. Good. 24. 1.00

510 —— *Sebastian I.*, 1557–78. 5 *Reis.* SEBASTIANVS I. D.G.P. ET ALGARBIORVM. Crowned arms. *Rev.*, REX SEXTVS DECIMVS. In field, large V. Good. 19. .75

511 —— *Peter II.* 1½ *Reis.* PETRVS D. G. PRINCEPS. Crowned arms. *Rev.*, PORTVGALIA, etc. In field, 1½. Poor. 16. .20

512 —— Same. 10 *Reis.* P. II. crowned in field. Leg. D. G. PORT ET ALG. REX. *Rev.*, VTILITATI PVBLICÆ, 1703. In field, large X. Fair. 23. .35

513 —— Same. 1703. 5 *Reis.* Type of last. *Rev.*, V. Good. 20. .40

514 —— Same. 1699. 3 *Reis.* Same type. *Rev.*, III , Fair. 17. .25

515 —— Same. 1699. 1½ *Reis.* Same type. *Rev.*, 1½. Fair. 15. .25

516 **Posen.** *Fred. Wm. III.* Eagle in an oval shield crowned. *Rev.*, 60 EINEN THALER | 3 | GROSCHEN | GR. HERZ | POSEN | 1816 | B(reslau). Good. 16. .25

517 ——— Same. *Rer.*, 180 Einen Thaler | 1 | Groschen | Gr. Herz | Posen | 1816 | A (m.m. of Berlin). Good. 13. .20

518 **Potosi,** La Union | es la | Fuerza | Potosi, 1864. *Rer.*, 1 | Centecl | mo. Fine. 13. .60

519 **Prussia,** *Fred. Wm. IV.*, 1864–68–47. 4-2-1 *Pfg.* Red, unc. 3 pes. .25

520 **Quedlinburg.** *Dorothea Sophia.* Pfennige. Shield of two parts. r. X l. E. Above is an ornament. *Rer.*, Imperial apple, dividing (16) 2–2. Good. 10. .25

521 **Ragusa,** *Follaro.* Racvsii Moneta. Laureated head l. *Rer.*, Civitas Racvsii. In field, a gateway with 3 towers. Good. 11. .25

522 ——— 6 *Veriers.* Prot. Reip. Rhacvsine. A saint standing, the head surrounded by the Nimbus, at his left a small gateway of 3 towers, on either side. 17–-05. *Rer.*, Devs Refvgi et Virtvs. St. Blasius standing. In ex., 6 (Soldo). Fair. 15. .35

523 ——— *Follaro.* Civitas Racvsii. Saint as above, behind the gateway. In ex. 1793. *Rer.*, The saint standing between two small crowned shields. Fair. 13. .20

524 **Ramleh,** (Palestine) Sug-el-Manscie Ramle. In field, 10 | Para | H.C.S. | 1863. *Rer.*, Turkish inscription. Brass. Good. 13. .40

525 **Ravenna,** *Benedict XIV.* 1740–58. Bened XIV. P. M. Arms, an oval shield of the bars surmounted by the Papal Keys and Tiara. *Rer.*, Un | Bajocco, within an ornamented shield. Pineapple at base. Good. 22. .50

526 ——— Same. *Quattrino.* Arms (alone) as on last. *Rer.*, S(anctus), A(pollinaris), P(rotector), Rav.(enna). The Saint standing. Fair. 12. .18

527 **Ravensburg.** The city gate between two towers. Above, the figure 4. (Heller) *Rer.*, Blank. Good. 9. .20

528 ——— 4 *Heller.* Gateway as before, dividing 16—96. *Rer.*, Blank. Good. 8. .25

529 **Reckheim,** *Ferdinand of Lyndon,* 1636–65, *Liard.* Ferdin et Elizabet. Crowned arms. *Rer.*, Com de Lin. Reck. In field, a cross between F. R., crowned. Good. 16. .35

530 ——— *Doit.* Arms in crowned shield supported by two lions. *Rer.*, Tra Rec.(heim). Fair. 13. .25

531 **Reggio,** *Hercules I.* 1471–1505, *Quattrino.* Hercles Dvx. Head l. *Rer.*, Regivm Olin Æmilia. Arms, a cross within a shield. Fair. 11. .25

532 ——— Same. *Quattrino.* Type of last. *Rer.*, Regivs Emelia Veteris. Arms as before. Fair. 11. .25

533 ——— *Hercules II.* 1534–58, *Quattrino.* Her. II. Dvx Regii IIII. Head l. *Rer.*, Re | givm | Lepi | di. Fair. 10. .25

534 ——— Same. *Quattrino.* S. Pro. Bust of St. Prospero full-face. *Rer.*, Regivm. Arms similar to 231. Good. 11. .25

535 **Riga,** *Christina.* 1532–54. Christina D. G. S. In field, the letter C. surrounding a bundle of arrows ; above, a crown. *Rer.*, Solidvs Civi Rig 6. 2 keys crossed : above, a small cross. Good. 9. .35

536 ——— *Chas. XI.* 1660-97. Carolvs Gvs. D. G. R. S. The letter G. within C., crowned. *Rer.*, Solidvs Civi Rigi 4. Keys as before. Good. 10. .40

537 **Roumania,** *Chas.* 1867. 1C-5-2-1 *Bani.* Red. Unc. 4 pcs. .70

538 **Rome,** *Leo. XII.* LEO. XII. P. M. A. III. Arms, Eagle in an oval shield surmounted by the Papal Keys and Tiara. *Rev.*, MEZZO | BAIOCO | ROM | 1826. Good. 17. .30

539 —— Same. AN. IV. *Rev.*, QVATRINO | ROM | 1826 | R. Good. 13. .20

540 —— *Pius VIII.* PIUS VIII PONT. MAX. ANNO. 1². Arms, a lion holding a castle l. etc. BAIOCCO | ROMANO | 1829. Fine. 21. .35

541 —— Same. *Rev.*, QVATTRINO | ROMANO | 1829. Good. 13 .20

542 —— *Gregory XVI.* GREGORIVS XVI. PONT. MAX. AN. 1. Arms in shield. *Rev.*,BAIOCCO | ROMANO | 1831. Good. 19. .25

543 —— Same. *Rev.*, MEZZO | BAIOCCO | ROMANO | 1831. Good. 15. .18

544 —— *Pius IX.* PIO IX P. M. View of the entrance of the Pantheon. *Rev.*, 10 | BAIOCCHI | ROMANI | 1848. To r. of date, Pantheon (as before) l. letter G. (aieta) crowned. Brass. Good. 12. 1.00

545 **Roman Republic,** 1798-99. REPVBBLICA ROMANA. Two flags a fasces. Liberty pole and cap crossed in field. In ex. T(omaso) M(creandetti Die cutter), in mon. Rev. DVE | BA | IOCCHI within a triangle. Branches crossed on either side. In ex. ANNO SESTO | REPVBBLI | CANO. Fine. 23. 1.50

546 —— Same. Legend as before. In field, the Roman eagle with outstretched wings perched upon a fasces. *Rev.*, DVE | BA | IOCCH I | within a triangle formed of 3 fasces. In ex. ANNO SESTO | REPVBB. Fine. 23. 1.25

547 —— Same. REPVBBLICA ROMANA. Fasces. In ex. T. M. *Rev.*, DVE | BAIOC | CHI. Fine. 23. .75

548 —— Same. Type of last. *Rev.*, VN | BAIOC | CO | R. Unc. 19. .75

549 —— Same. Type of last. *Rev.*, MEZZO | BAIOCCO. Fair. 16. .55

550 —— 1849. DIO E POPOLO. The Roman eagle perched upon a fasces, within a heavy wreath of oak. In ex. R.(oma). *Rev.*, REPUBBLICA ROMANA. In field, 3 | BAIOCCHI. In ex. 1849. Good. 24. .40

551 —— Same. 1 *Baiocco.* Good. 19. .35

552 —— Same. ½ *Baiocco.* Good. 16. .30

553 **Ruremond.** *Albert and Elisabeth.* LIARD. ALBERTVS ET ELIS. D. G. Crowned arms (of Burgundy, etc.) *Rev.*, ARCHI DVCES. AVS DVC. GEL. (rae). In field, a shield bearing a lion and a crown in centre of a cross : in the angles, a crown, a fleece and the date, 1600. Fair. 17. .20

554 —— *Chas. II.*—DEMI LIARD. CAR. II. D. G. HISP. REX. Crowned arms. *Rev.*, shield and cross, as in last. Dividing date, 16-61. Poor. 12. .15

555 **Russia.** *Peter* the Great, 1711 (in Russian). *Copeck.* Horse with rider l. INs. in Russian, Struck at Moscow. Good. 16. .50

556 —— *Alexander I.* 5 KOPECKS. The Russian imperial double eagle crowned within a band of 5 circles. *Rev.*,5 | KOPECKS (latter in Russian characters). 1803 | E.(katerinburg) M. (Mint), within a band of 5 circles. Good. Thick. 27. .45

557 —— *Nicholas I.* Russian imperial double eagle crowned in field. In ex. 1837. *Rev.*,10 | KOPECKS (latter is Russian). In ex. m. m., E. M. Fair. 27. .35

558 **St. Enstasins,** (West India Island). God Bless St. Eusta-
tius & Guvs. In field, a gosling eating grass. *Rer.*,
Herman Gossling. 1771. In field, 1 Bt. Brass. Fine.
15. 2.25

559 **St. Gall,** Canton St. Gallen. A fasces in a shield between
sprigs of-laurel. In ex. 1815. *Rer.*, I | Bazen. Base.
Good, 16. .18

560 **St. Thomas,** 80 *Reis*. Pecunia Totum Circumit Orbem.
The arms of Portugal within a square shield upon a globe.
*Rer.*, Joannes VI. D. G. Port. Bras. et Alg. Rex. In
field, 80 | 1825. Crowned. At either side of the denomi-
nation, an open flower. Good. 23. .60

561 —— Same. 40 *Reis*. 1821. Fine. 19. .40

562 —— Same. 20 *Reis*. 1825. Good. 16. .30

[Note.—The island of St. Thomas lies directly on the equator, about
150 miles from the Congo Coast, Africa. It must not be confoun-
ded with the West India Island of the same name, It was discovered
by the Portugese on St. Thomas' Day, 1471. Its principal town is
Povoasao. These pieces are distinguished by the plain figures (not
numerals) of the denomination on the reverse; also by the open flower
on either side of the same, just as those struck by Portugal for use
in the Azores are distinguished by the ornamented figures used to
denote the denomination, and the bunches of flowers with which the
arms are draped.]

563 **San Domingo,** F. Y. Crowned. *Rer.*, S. D. ¼ (Real). Fair.
15. .75

564 —— S. D. Beneath, a fish. *Rer.*, a large anchor. Lead.
Fair. 14. 1.00

565 **San Jose.** San José, C.(osta) R.(ica). *Rer.*, Escojida de
Cafe. Brass. Unc. 14. A coffee-house check or token.
.18

566 **Sans Luis Potosi.** Mexico Libre. An Indian seated,
holding in the right hand an arrow, upon which is a liberty
cap. To r. a cornucopia; l. a cactus plant. *Rer.*, Estado
Libre de San Luis Potosi. In field, ¼ (Real). Above,
an open book. In ex. 1860. Fair. 18. .65

567 **San Marino.** Repubblica di S. Marino. Three castles
upon three mountain peaks, in an oval shield, crowned.
Below the shield upon a ribbon is the word Libertas,
incused. In ex. Gori (Die sinker). *Rer.*, 10 | Centesimi
| 1875. In ex. a fasces. Good. 19. .85

568 —— Same. Legend and arms as last. In ex. a star. *Rer.*,
5 | Centesimi | 1869. In ex. m. m., M. (ilan). Good. 16.
.30

569 **San Severino,** 2½ *Baiocchi*, S(anctus) P(etrus). Apostolorom
Princeps. Bust of St. Peter, l. Head surrounded by a
Nimbus and holding the keys of Heaven. *Rer.*, Baiocchi
| Dve e Mezzo | S. Severino | 1796. Good. 19. .45

570 **Santa Martha,** ¼ *Real*, ¼ crowned. Dividing a castle, a
cannon and six cannon balls. In ex. 1820. *Rer.*, a cross
in the angles S(anta) M(arta), and two ornaments. Fine,
of rude workmanship. 14. .40

571 —— F. VII., within a circle of pellets. *Rer.*, S. M. within a
similar circle. Fair. 13. .60

572 **Sandwich Islands.** Kamehameha III. Ka Moi. Bust in
military dress ; full face. In ex. 1847. *Rer*, Aupuni
Hawaii. In field, Hapa Haneri. Red. Unc. 18. .90

573 **Sarawak,** J. Brooke, Rajah. Head l. *Rer.*, Sarawak 1863.
In field, One | Cent. Fine. 19. .65

574 —— Same. *Half-Cent.* Good. 15. .55

575 —— Same. ¼ *Cent.*] [Fair. 11. .50

576 —— C. Brooke Rajah. Head l. *Rev.*, Sarawak 1870. In
field, One Cent. Good. 19.                          .65
577 —— Same. Half-Cent. Good. 15.                   .55
578 —— Same. 1/4 Cent. Good. 11.                     .60
579 **Sardinia,** *Victor Amadeus* Vic. Am. D. G. R Sar. Cyp. et
Ier. Bust r. *Rev.*, Dvx Sab. et Montis f. Princ Ped.
1724. The Sardinian cross. In the angles 4 heads facing
l. Fair. 11.                                        .20
580 —— Same. A cord tied in a loose knot of two bows, crowned.
In ex. 1725. *Rev.*, Vic Am. D. G. Sar. Ie. et Cy. e D.
Sa. Mfs. P. Pe. The Sardinian cross. Fine. 9.      .18
581 —— *Charles Emanuel.* Car. E. m. D. G. Rex. Sar. Cyp(rus)
et Ier(Jerusalem). Bust r. *Rev.*, Dvx Sab.et Montis f.
Princ. Ped. 1741. The Sardinian cross as in No. 579,
dividing 3-C(avalli). Good. 15.                    .25
582 —— *Victor Amadeus II.* Vic. Am. D. G. R. Sa.(rdinia)
Cy.(prus) *et Je* (Jerusalem), 1781. The Piedmontese cross.
*Rev.*, Dvx Sal. et Montisf. Pr. Ped. V. A. in mon.
crowned, dividing M(ezzo). S(oldo). Fair. 11.      .18
583 —— Same. *Mezzo Soldo.* Knot and crown as in No. 580. In ex.,
1784. *Rev.*, Vic. Am. D. G. R. Sar, Cyp. et. Ier. D. Sab.
et Mf. P. P. The Sardinian cross. Good. 10.        .15
584 —— Same. *Mezzo Soldo.* The knot within a wreath. *Rev.*, Vic.
Am. D. G. Rex. Sar., 1788. The Sardinian cross ; in the
angle, 4 heads facing r. Good. 10.                 .20
585 —— *Charles Emanuel IV.* The knot and crown as in 580.
In ex., 1800. *Rev.*, Carolvs Em. Iv. D. G. Rex. Sar.
Cyp. et Ier. The Sardinian cross. Good. 11         .18
586 —— *Charles Felix,* 1826. 5. 3 and 1 centesimi. Red. Unc.
3 pcs.                                             .45
589 **Savoy,** *Charles II.*, 1504-53. *Parpajola.* Car. S. Rom. Dvx
Sab. The Savoyard cross in a shield. *Rev.*, in field, a
cross, with small crown on each arm. Poor. 12.     .15
590 —— Same. The Savoyard cross. Crowned. *Rev.*, the Piedmontese cross. With two Cs interlined in the angles.
Poor. 10.                                          .15
591 —— *Charles Emanuel.* Parpajola. Carols Emanvel.
*Rev.*, the cross in a shield. Dvx Sabavdie, 1582. The
Piedmontese cross, with four triangular ornaments in
the angles. Fair. 12.                              .25
592 —— Same. *Soldo.* Car Em. D. G. The Pascal Lamb,
carrying a banner bearing the cross. *Rev.*, Mihi,——1623.
The Piedmontese cross. Poor. Clipped. 10.          .15
593 —— Same *Sesino.* C.(arlovs) E.(manvel). Crowned.
*Rev.*, The Piedmontese cross. In ex. C. Good. 9.
                                                   .18
594 —— Same. *S. Soldi.* Car. Em. D. G. Dvx. Sab. P. Ped. e
C. Bust, with large ruffle r. In ex., 1626. *Rev.*, in Hoc.
Ego. S. Pera. Bo. The Savoyard cross in a crowned
shield, on either side the outer arms of the Piedmontese
cross. Good. 16.                                   .35
595 —— Same. *Parpajola.* Car. Em. D. G. Vx. Sab. Bust
r. *Rev.*, Carol E. Avg. The cross in a crowned shield.
In ex., 1630. Fair. 12.                            .20
596 —— *Charles Emanuel II.*, 1637-75. Car.——Sab. Cross in a
shield, on either side the letters F. E. R. T. *Rev.*, Gloria
——. The Piedmontese cross. Fair. Clipped. 8.       .20
597 —— Same. Soldo. Ca. Em. D. G. R. Sa. Salvs Mvndi.
The Piedmontese cross. Fair. 10.                   .20
598 —— *Victor Amedeus Francesco.* Vic. Am. II. D. G. Dvx.
Sab. The Savoyard cross. In the angles, 4 lilies. *Rev.*,
Prin. Pede. Rex. Cyp. V. A. in crowned mon. dividing
date, 16-88. Good. 13.                             .25

599 **Sayn Wittgenstein.** A crowned shield of two parts. R.
a lion rampant, l. an eagle. *Rev.*, ¼ | STVBER | 1753.
Good 14. .18
600 —— Same. *Rev.*, 1 | PFENNING | 1853. Fair. 11. .18
601 **Saxony.** Crowned arms between palm branches. *Rev.*, 1 |
HELLER | 1799 | E. Red. Unc. 11. .25
602 —— K. S. S. M. Crowned Arms. *Rev.*, 2 | PFENNIGE |
1856 | F. Also 1 *Pfg.* 1859. Red. Unc. 2 pcs. .30
603 **Saxon-Meiningen.** A (NTON) V (LRICH) in crowned mon.
*Rev.*, 3 | HELLER | 1761. .18
604 —— A hen crowned r. *Rev.*, 1 | MEININ | HELLER | 1762.
Poor. .15
605 **Schaumberg.** A shield within 3 nettle leaves, within an orna-
mented oval. *Rev.*, 1 | PFENNING | SCHEIDE | MVNTZ |
1750. Fair. 14. .18
606 **Schoonhaven,** S.(tuber) VI within three circles. *Rev.*,
Incused. Fair. 14. 1.00
607 **Schweenfurt.** An eagle in a shield dividing S.—M. 16—22
above S. *Rev.*, 84 within a wreath. Fine. 11. .40
608 **Schwyz.** An oval shield within a shell. In the upper r.
corner a cross. *Rev.*, 1 | RAPPEN | 1846. Good. 11. .18
609 **Servia,** *Michael III.* Inscription in Russian. Head r. 10 | PARA
(in Russian) | 1868. Above, a crown. Red. Unc. 20. .40
610 —— Same. 5 *Para.* 1868. Fine. 16. .25
611 —— Same. 1 *Para.* 1868. Red. Unc. 10. .25
612 **Siam,** ¼ *Fuang.* Inscription in Siamese. A pagoda with
radiated spire. *Rev.*, Inscription. Unc. 13. 30
613 **Siberia,** Catherine II. 1781. 10 *Kopecks.* Two sables supporting crowned shield. *Rev.*, E (katarine) II. in mon.
Crowned. Good. 29. 1.25
614 **Sicily,** *Roger,* Count, 1085-1101. ROGERIVS COMES. The
Count mounted l. holding a large banner and a buckler.
*Rev.*, MARIA MATER DNI. The Virgin seated upon a
chair holding the Infant Jesus. Good. 18. .60
615 —— *John II.,* King, 1458-79, IOAN(nes) D. G. C. An eagle.
*Rev.*, a shield surmounted by a cross. REX SICILIE.
Fair. 9. .20
616 —— Same, but smaller and of different workmanship.
Good. 7. .20
617 —— *Frederic III.,* 1486—1501. FEDERICVS DEI G. REX. SI
IIE. (rusalem) Crowned arms. *Rev.*, VICTORIE FRVCTVS.
Two cornucopias joined. Fair. 16. 30
618 —— *Philip II.* 2 *Grana.* PHILIPP D. G. REX ARA (gon)
VTR. Head crowned r. *Rev.*, PVBLICA COMODITATI. In
field, a bunch of grapes dividing date, 15—88. Good.
17. .40
619 —— *Philip IV.* 5 *Grana.* PHILIPPVS IIII. D. G. 1625. Bust
l. To r. of bust the letter M. C. *Rev.*, PVBLI | CA |
COMMO | DITAS. Fair. 21. .40
620 —— Same. 4 *Cavalli,* PHILIPPVS IIII. D. G. R. Bust r.
To right, the letters C. A, | C, l. I Ex. 1638. *Rev.*, A fleece
suspended. Good, but somewhat clipped. 16. .40
621 —— Same. 4 *Cavalli.* Type of preceding. To r. of bust
the letter S.: 1662 in legend. *Rev.*, Fleece as before.
Fair. 15. .35
622 —— *Charles II.* 2 *Tornesi.* CAROLVS II. D. G. REX. Bust
r. To right letter S.; l. A. C. | A. In ex. (16)79. *Rev.*,
SICIL ET IIERVSA. A shield of two parts ; r., a Jerusalem Cross ; l. 2 eagles and 8 bars. Crowned. Good. 18.
.50

623 ——— Same. 2 *Tornesi.* Type of last. Letters 1. of bust, A.
C. | A. In ex. (16)80. *Rev.*, same as last. Fair. 18. 40.

624 ——— *Ferdinand IV. Ferdinan IV.* Sici Rex. Head r. In
ex. P. *Rev.*, A cross with end in form of fleur-de-lis,
dividing C(avalli) 3. In ex. 1789. Good. 11. .20

625 ——— Same. Ferdinan IV. D. G. Rex. Bust r. *Rev.* A
fortress, dividing C(avallos). 9. In ex. 1804. Fine. 16.
.40

626 ——— *Joachim Napoleon.* (Murat.) Gioacchino Nap. Re
Delle Due Sic. Head 1. *Rec.*, Prin e Grand, Ammi
di Fran. In field, 3 | Grana. In ex. 1810. Good. 21.
.65

627 ——— Same. Gioacchino Napoleone. Re delle Due Sici.
Head 1. *Rev.*, Prin e Grand, Ammi di Fran. In field,
Grana | 2. In ex. 1810. Poor. 18. .25

628 ——— *Ferdinand IV.* Ferdinandus IV. D. G. Sicil Rex.
Head r. *Rev.*, Otto—Tornesi | 1816. Red. Unc. 22.
.60

629 ——— *Ferdinand I.* (Same as Ferd. IV.) Ferd. I. D. G.
Regni Siciliarvm et Hier, Rex. Head crowned 1.
*Rev.*, Quattro | Tornesi | 1817. Red. Unc. 18. .45

630 ——— **and Naples.** *William II.* 1166–89. *Part Fallaro.* An
Arabic legend in the Cufic characters reading. *Struck by
the order of the Magnificent King who put his glory in God.*
In field, *The King William II. Rev..* Operata in Vrbe
Messane. In field, Rex. W. | S.C.&.S. Good, but a
little clipped. 9. .70

631 ——— Same. The head of a lion full face. *Rev..* Arabic inscription, reading, *The King William II.* Good. 8. .55
[Note.—The appearance of the Arabic language upon Sicilian coins
needs, perhaps, a word of explanation to those who are not familiar
with the early history of the island. Sicily was conquered by the
Aghlabe Caliphs A. II., 216 (A. D, 838). At that time they had made
themselves masters of the whole of Northern Africa, also of Spain,
Sardinia and Malta, and had even invaded the suburbs of Rome.
They were succeeded by the Fatimite Dynasty, who, with some
changes, held Sicily until it was wrested from them by Roger the
Norman in 1085, who then became Count of Sicily, his son, Roger II.
being declared king in 1130. During the two centuries of Mahom-
medan rule the Arabic language came into general use, so much so
that it was for many years considered necessary to use it on the
coinage. This practice ceased, however, at the beginning of the 13th
century.

632 ——— *Charles II.* (of Anjou). 1285-1309. *Denaro.* Karol
Scd Rex. Bust crowned, full face. *Rec.*, Ierl et Sicil.
Arms, 4 lilies upon a lambel (the arms of Anjou). Poor.
9. .35

633 ——— *Ferdinand I.*, 1458-79. *Carallo.* Ferdinandvs Rex.
Bust crowned r. *Rev.*, Eqvitas Regni. A horse stepping r.; before him an eagle. Good. 12. .25

634 ——— *Ferdinand II.*, 1495-96. Ferdinandvs D. G. R. The
King seated upon two lions holding a sceptre and the
crucifixial globe. *Rer.*, Sicilie Iervsal. Jerusalem
cross. Good. 10. .40

635 ——— *Frederic III.*, 1496-1501. *Carallo.* Leticia Popvli. The
letter F crowned dividing two ornaments. *Rer.*, Ivstvs
Rex. Jerusalem cross. Poor. 13. .20

636 ——— Same. *Carallo.* Federicvs Rex. Head crowned r.
*Rer.*, Eqvitas Regni. A horse stepping r., above him a
star of 7 points. In ex., L. star at either side. Good.
Clipped. 10. .18

637 ——— *Charles IV. and Johanna*, 1516-17. *Grano.* Leticia
Popvli. In field, the letters I. C.|crowned. *Rer.*, Ivstvs
Rex. Jerusalem cross. Poor. 13. .15

638 —— Same. *Grano.* PLVS VLTRA The Pillars of Hercules, united by a band, crowned and resting on the sea. *Rer.,* IVSTVS REX. Jerusalem cross. Good. 11. .35

639 —— *Philip IV.* 4 *Tornesi* PHILIPP IIII., D. G. 1622. Bust crowned l. To right the letters M. C. *Rer.,* —— NAPOLIS REX. ——. In field, a Jerusalem cross with 4 crosslets in the angles. Fair. Clipped. 18. .35

640 **Siebenburgen.** A crowned shield of two parts between palm and laurel branches. Upper, the head and wings of an eagle, a star and a crescent; lower, 7 towers in two lines. *Rer.,* EIN | GRESCHL | 1764. Good. 14. .25

641 **Sienna,** *Quattrino.* XV. century. SENAVETVS. In field, the letter S ornamented. *Rev.,* CIVITAS VIRG.(inis). Before the legend a small crucifixial globe. In field, an ornamented cross. Poor. 11. .15

642 **Sierra Leone,** SIERRA LEONE COMPANY. A lion facing l. his tail upraised. In ex. AFRICA. *Rev.,* ONE CENT PIECE. 1791. The hand of a white and a black clasped. Above and below, the figure 1. Bronze proof. 18. 1.00

643 **Silesia,** *Frederic William I.* (of Prussia). F. W. beneath a crown. *Rec.,* ¼ | KREUZER | SCHLES LAND | MUNZE | 1797 | B. Fair. 14. .18

644 —— An eagle within a crowned oval shield between branches of oak. *Rev,* NEUNZIG EINEN REICHS THALER | 1 | KREUTZER | SCHLES | 1810 | A. Fair. 15. .18

645 **Sinaloa,** ESTADO LIBRE Y SOBRANO DE SINALOA. Liberty head between laurel branches. *Rer.,* ¼ | DE REAL | 1848. Fair. 16. .45

646 —— Same. 1861. ¼ *Real.* Fair. 16 .35

647 —— Same. 1862. ¼ *Real.* Good 16. .40

648 **Solothurn** (Swiss Canton). SOLODORENSIS. A small shield dividing S. O. *Rer.,* MONETA REIP. 1797. In field, an an ornamented cross. Good. 10. .15

649 **Sonora,** ESTO LIBRE Y SOBO, DE SONORA. Eagle upon cactus. *Rer.,* UNA CUARTILLA DE REAL. 1859. Liberty seated, holding a cap upon a pole, at her feet a cornucopia. 21. .50

650 **Spain,** *Charles III.* 8 *Mararedis,* CAROLVS III. D. G. HISP. REX. Head r. dividing a castle and the figure 8 (Maravedis). In ex. 1785. *Rer.,* the arms of Spain. 2 lions and castles divided by a cross, in the centre of which is a shield bearing 4 lilies. Good. 19. .45

651 —— *Charles IV.* 4 *Mararedis,* CAROLVS IIII. D. G. HISP. REX. Head r. dividing a castle and the figure 4. In ex. 1806. *Rer.,* arms of Spain. Brass. Fair. 14. .75
The only one in this metal I have met with. It *is not* a cast.

652 —— *Joseph Napoleon.* 8 *Maravedis,* JOSEPH NAP. REX DE HISP. Head l. dividing 8. M(aravedis). In ex. 1812. Segovia m m. above. *Rer.,* The arms of Spain, as in No. 650; in the central shield the imperial French eagle instead of the 3 lilies of the Bourbons. Fair. 19. 2.50

653 —— *Ferdinand VII.* FERDIN. VII. D. G. ET C. HISP REX. Head l. dividing P(ampeluna).—8 (Maravedis). Ex. 1823. *Rer.,* the arms of Spain, as in No. 650. An uncirculated original cast in gun metal, in the bold, rude workmanship so common on Spanish coins of that period. 18. 2.00

654 —— Same. 8 *Maravedis.* FERDIN. VII. D. G. HISP. REX. Head r. dividing J. 8. In ex. 1824. *Rer.,* arms of Spain, as before. Fine. 18. .45

655 —— Same. 1833. Type of last. 4 *Mararedis.* Good. 15. .25

656 —— Same. 1833. Type of last. 2 *Maravedis.* Good. 12. .18

64

657 —— *Isabel II.* 8 MARAVEDIS. ISABEL 2ᴬ POR LA GRACIA DE DIOS. Bust r. In ex. 1835. *Rev.*, REYNA DE ESPAÑA Y DE LAS INDIAS 8—M(aravedis). Separated by m. m. J. (ubia). The arms of Spain. Fine. 18. .40

658 —— Same. 1 *Maravedi.* ISABEL 2ᴬ POR LA G. DE DIOS Y LA CONST. Head r. dividing 1—M. In ex. 1842. *Rev.*, REYNA DE LAS ESPANAS. The arms of Spain. Unc. Partly red. 9. .40

659 —— Same. ISABEL 2ᴬ FOR LA G. DE DIOS. The arms of Spain within a crowned and ornamented shield. *Rev.*, Y LA CONST. REINA DE LAS ESPAÑAS. 1848. In field, MEDIO | REAL | CINCO | DECIMAS | M. Good. 20. .60

660 —— Same. 8 *Maravedis.* ISABEL 2ᴬ POR LA G. DE DIOS Y. LA CONST. Head r., dividing 8.—M. In ex. 1855. *Rev.*, REYNA DE LAS ESPAÑAS. Arms of Spain. In ex., BA(rcelona). Very good. 19. .30

661 —— *Charles VII.* (Don Carlos, the Pretender). CARLOS VII., P. L. GRACIA DE DIOS REY DE LAS ESPAÑAS. Head laureated r. Beneath, O. 1. (initials of die-cutter). *Rev.*, 10 CENTIMOS DE PESETA. The arms of Spain within a crowned shield. Beneath, laurel branches. On either side, C. 7 in crowned mon. In ex., 1875, between a flower and a fleur-de-lis. Good. 19. 2.00
[NOTE.—Of this piece, struck by the unfortunate Don Carlos, it is unnecessary to say a word, the events which it commemorates being of too recent date to have been forgotten by anyone. It is of the highest interest and rarity.]

662 **Speyer.** A shield bearing a cross and a smaller shield of two bars, surmounted by a cardinal's hat, the pendants of which form the supporters. Behind the shield a sword and a crosier. In ex., B(ishopric) S(peyer). *Rev.*, 1 | KREUTZER | LAND MUNZ | 1765. Good. 16. .35

663 —— Same type as last *Rev.*, II PFENNIG | LAND MUNZ | 1765. Fair. 14. .30

664 **Straits Settlements,** VICTORIA QUEEN. Bust crowned l. *Rev.*, ONE | CENT | INDIA | STRAITS | 1862. Fair. 18. .20

665 —— Same. *Half cent.* Fair. 15. .25

666 —— Same. ¼ *cent.* Fair. 11. .30

667 —— VICTORIA QUEEN. Head, very different from No. 664, crowned, r. Under the head, H(eaton). *Rev.*, STRAITS SETTLEMENTS ONE CENT. 1872. In field, 1. Unc. Partly red. 18. .30

668 —— Same. *Rev.*, STRAITS SETTLEMENTS. HALF CENT. 1872. In field, ½. Good. 15. .25

669 **Stollberg.** A stag, with its horns locked in a column, which is surmounted by the crucifixial globe. Upon the base of the column is inscribed the letter S(tollberg). *Rev.*, 1½ | PFENNIG | SCHEIDE | MUNTZ | 1722. Fair 14. .20

670 —— Same type. *Rev.*, 1 | PFENNIG | SCHE DE | MUNTZ | 1722. Good. 12. .20

671 **Suriname** (Dutch Guiana), 4 *Doits.* A paroquet perched upon a branch. Behind his head the figure 4. (Doits.) In ex., AN. 1679. *Rev.*, blank. Good. 13 .75

672 —— Type of last. 2 *Doits.* Behind the paroquet's head the figure 2. (Doits.) *Rev.*, blank. Good. 11. 1.00

673 —— *Doit.* A coffee shrub dividing date, 17—64. *Rev.*, SOCIETEIT VAN SURINAME. Good. 12. .40

674 **Sweden,** *Charles XI.* Three crowns on either side the letters C(arolus) R(ex) S(verige). In ex., 16—83, divided by a star. *Rev.*, crowned lion rampant l., dividing ⅛—Oᴿ S.—M. Fair. 15. .40

675 —— *Charles XII.* 3 crowns. Above, C. XII, in mon. R(ex) S(verige). In ex. 1708. Crowned lion rampant l. dividing ⅙—Or. S.—M. Good. 15. .25

676 —— Same. 1718. Arrangement of crowns similar to last. *Rev.*, Lion rampant l. in a crowned shield of three bars, dividing ⅙—Or. S.—M. Good. 15. .20

677 —— Same, (period of ministry of Baron de Goertz), a large crown surmounted by a cross ; beneath, 1715. *Rev.*, 1 | Daler | S. M. Good. 15. .25

678 —— Same. Pvblica Fide. A female seated l. holding in her right hand a leaf, her left supporting a spear and a shield bearing the 3 crowns. In ex. 1716. *Rev.*, 1 | Daler | S. M. Good. 15. .25

679 —— Same. Wett och Wapen. (Cunning and brave.) A Warrior with sword and shield, the latter bearing the three crowns. In ex. 1717. *Rev.*, ¹ | Daler | S. M. within a shield. Above a lion's head; at either side, flags, pikes and spears, beneath two cornucopias. Fair. 15. .25

680 —— Same. Flink Och Fardig. (Quick and ready.) A warrior holding sword and spear by the side of a lion, both advancing l. In ex. 1718. *Rev.*, 1 | Daler | S, M. In a shield, supported by two cornucopias, flags, cannon, pikes and spears. Fair. 15. .18

681 —— Same. Ivpiter. Jupiter standing holding the thunder-bolt. At his feet the eagle. In ex. 1718. 1 | Daler | S. M. Within a circle formed of 3 crowns and 4 branches of laurel. Fair. 15. .25

682 —— Same. Mars. The God of War, standing l. holding a spear and shield. In ex. 1718. *Rev.*, 1 | Daler | S. M. within a crown and ornamented circle. Fair. 15. .30

683 —— Same. Mercvrivs. Mercury holding his serpent wand l. In ex. 1718. *Rev.*, 1 | Daler | S. M., within an or-namented shield. Good. 15. .25

684 —— Same. Phœbvs. The God of the Morning standing within a radiated circle (representing sunrise), holding in his right hand a wand surmounted by the blazing sun. In ex. 1718. *Rev.* 1 | Daler | S. M , within an ornamen-ted circle. Good. 15. .25

685 —— Same. Satvrnvs. Saturn, the God of Time advancing l. holding in his right hand an infant which he is about to devour, his left supporting a scythe. In ex. 1718. *Rev.*, 1 | Daler | S. M., within a floral circle. Fair. 15. .25

686 —— Same. Hoppet. The goddess Hope, standing upon an anchor. In ex. 1719. 1 | Daler | S. M., within an or-namented circle. Fair. 15. .20

687 —— *Gustavus III.* G(vstavus) R(ex) S(verige) above 3 crowns. In ex. 1772. 2 arrows crossed within a crown-ed shield dividing 1 Or. K. M. Fair. 15. .40

688 **Tarragona,** De : Ta : ra : go : na. In field, a checkered shield. *Rev.*, the letter T within an ornamented circle. Fair. 16. .65

689 **Tepic** (Mexico), An eagle with outstretched wings. Above, a star of six points dividing B.—P. Incused. *Rev.*, Blank. Brass. 16. A Token for ¼ Real issued by Boni-facio Peña, between 1850 and 1857. 1.00

690 **Thorn,** *Livrd,* Anna D Marck ab Th(oren). A crowned shield bearing 2 lions, 3 crescents, 3 fleur-de-lis and 3 bars. Sit No Domini Benedi. A cross formed of 4 fleur-de-lis crowned, dividing 16-14. Good. 17. .50

691 **Ticino** Cantone Ticino, 1835. A circular shield, enclosed within a wreath, made up of fine lines, to r. running hori-zontally, to l. perpendicularly. *Rev.*, Denari | Tve. In ex. laurel branches crossed. Good. 10. .20

692 **Tournay.** *Philip IV.* (of Spain), *Liard* (or 12 myten) Phs. D.
G. Hisp. Z Rex. D. Torn. Bust crowned l. In ex. a
small castle (m. m. of Tournay) dividing (15) 8–5. *Rev.*,
Dominvs Mihi Adivtor. Crowned shield of four quarterings containing : lower r., lion rampant l.; upper r.,
3 leaves ; upper l., 3 bars ; lower l., 3 pales. In centre,
small lion rampant l. Good. 16.                      .45

693 —— *Albert and Elizabeth*, Liard. Albertvs Elisabeth Dei
Gratia. Crowned arms, dividing 16—11. *Rev.*, Arch
Avst. Dvces Bvrg Dom. Tor. 3 shields and two
crowns in form of a cross. Fair. 16.                 .20

694 —— *Obsidional.* 8 *Stubers.* Crowned shield between palm
branches bearing 3 ornaments, dividing 8—S(tubers).
*Rev.*, Moneta | In | obsIDione | TornaCensi CVsa.
Fair. 19.                                          1.00

695 —— Same. *Liard* of John Louis of Eldern, Archbishop of
Liege counterstamped Obsesso Tornaco. In field, a
a castle, above which is the figure 2 (Patards) beneath the
date 1709. Good. 15.                                .75

696 **Trinidad.** One | Farthing | Token. *Rev.*, Redeemable
by J. G. D'Ade & Co. | Trinidad. Good. 13.       1.00

697 **Tuscany,** *Cosmus III.*, 3 *Quattrini*, Ovattrini. Six pellets
crowned. In ex. III. (Quattrini). *Rev.*, a cross dividing
in ex. 16–81. Fair. 13.                             .30

698 —— Same. 2 *Quattrini*. Qvattrini. Arms as last. In
ex. II. (Quattrini). *Rev.*, same as last, date being 16–89.
Fair. 11.                                           .25

699 —— *Ferdinand III.* Ferd. III. A. A. M. D. et R. *Rev.*,
Crowned shield bearing the Arms of Tuscany, r. 6 pellets l., 3 daggers, in centre 6 bars divided into 2 groups.
*Rev.*, Qvat | trino | 1792. Fine. 10.              .25

700 —— Same. Type of last. *Rev.*, Qvat | trino | 1796. Poor.
10.                                                 .12

701 —— Same. Ferd. III. A. D. A. G. D. Di Tosc. Arms as
above, in oval crowned shield. In ex. 8 and a small
hammer. *Rev.*, Un Ventesimo di Lira. In field.
Soldo. In ex. 1822. Fine. 12.                       .30

702 **Tuxpango,** 10 *Centavos.* An eagle upon a cactus killing a
snake. *Rev.*, Hacienda de Tuxpango, Mexico. In
field, 10. Brass. Good. 19.                         .75

703 **Ulm.** An ornamented 2 part, oval shield, upper sable, lower
plain above, Ulm. *Rer.*, Ein | Kreutzer | 1773. Good.
15.                                                 .25

704 **Urbino,** *Guido Ubaldo I.*, 1482-1508. Duke *Quattrino*, Gvidvs
Vb. Vrb. Dv. Bust, with long flowing hair, l. *Rev.*,
Com. Mon. Fe. Ec. Dvrant. Shield above a crown,
bearing upon it an eagle, fleur-de-lis, 2 pales, bunch of
grapes, etc. Poor. 12.                              .18

705 **Valencia.** Archduke Philip IV., 1621–65. Philippvs D. G.
Head r. *Rer.*, Valen-cio. Poor 11.                 18

706 **Venice,** *Antonio Venieri*, 1382-1400. *Matapane.* Vexilifer
Venetiar. The winged lion of St. Mark holding the
book of the Evangelists. *Rer.*, Anto Venerio Dvx.
In field, a cross. Fair. 10.                        .25
[Note.—The *Matapan* is properly a silver coin of about the same
size as this piece. This Doge alone seems to have made them of
copper.]

707 —— *Francesco Foscari*, 1423-57. *Piccolo.* Fra. Fo. Dvx.
In field, a cross. *Rer.*, Lion passing to left between the
letters S.(an) M.(arcus). Fair. Clipped. 6.         .13

708 —— *Nicolas Tronus*, 1471-73. *Sesino*. NICOLAVS TRONVS DVX. Bust left. *Rev.*, SANCTVS MARCVS. The winged lion walking 1. carrying a banner. Fair. 12. .40

709 —— *Giovanni Mocenigo*, 1478-85. *Bagattino*. IOANES MOCENIGO DVX. The doge kneeling r, holding a banner dividing the letters F. F. *Rev.*, the winged lion of St. Mark holding the book of the Evangelists Brass. Thick. Good. 11. .50

710 —— *Sebastiano Vanier*, 1577-78. *Bagattino*. SEB. VENERIVS DVX VENE. A cross surrounded by 16 pellets. *Rev.*, the lion as before. SANCTVS MARCVS VENETVS. Fair. 12. .50

711 —— *Pasquale Cicogna*, 1585-95. *Quattrino*. PASC. CICONIA DVX VEN. Cross as in last. *Rev.*, same as last. Fair. 11. .20

712 —— *Marino Grimani*, 1595-1606. *Quattrino*. MARINVS GRIMAN. DVX. Cross as in No. 710. *Rev.*, similar to No. 710. Fair. 12. .25

713 —— *Antonio Priuli*, 1618-23. *Soldo* (or 12 Deniers). S(anctvs) M(arcvs) VE(netvs) ANT. PRI The Doge holding a cross and facing the winged lion of St. Mark. In ex. 12 (Deniers). *Rev.*, DEFENSO NOSTER. St. Mark standing. Good. 14. .30

714 —— Same. *Half Soldo*. Type of last. (With 6 *Deniers*.) Fine. 12. .50

715 —— Same. *Quattrino*. ANTON PRIOLI DVX VEN. A cross surrounded by 16 pellets. *Rev.*, same as No. 710. Fair. 11. .18

716 —— Same. *Bagattino*. ANT. PR. DVX VEN. A cross. In the angles, 4 stars. *Rev.*, S. MARCVS VEN. The head of the saint within a circle Good. 8. .30

717 —— *Giovanni Cornaro*. *Soldo*. S. M. VE. IO. CORN. Type of No. 713. Fair. 14. .25

718 —— *Nicolas Contarini*, 1630-31. *Soldo*. S. M. V. NIC. CON. Type of No. 713 Fair. 14. .65
[Note.—The short reign of one year of this Doge render all his coins rare. Neither the Morbion or Rossi collection of Italian coins contained a *specimen* of his money.]

719 —— *Francesco Erizzo*, 1631-46. *Soldo*. S. M. V. FRANC. ERI. Type of No. 713. Fair. 15. .25

720 —— *Carlo Contarini*. 1655-56. *Soldo*. S. M. V. CAROL CONTA. Type of No. 713. Poor. 15. .50

721 —— *Bertuccio Valeri*, 1656-58. *Soldo*. S. M. V. BERT. VALER. Type of No. 713. Poor. 15. .45

722 —— *Nicolas Sagredo*, 1675-76. *Soldo*. S. M. V. NI. SAGRED. Type of No. 713. Fair. 15. .60
[NOTE.—The money of the three preceding Doges, is from the same cause as in the case of Nicolas Contarini, exceedingly difficult to obtain. The Morbio Collection contained no specimen of the coinage of either.]

723 —— *Aloys Contarini*, 1676-84. *Soldo*. S. M. V. ALOYS CON. D. Type of No. 713. Good. 15. .40

724 —— *Marco-Antonio Giustiniani*, 1684-88. *Soldo*. S. M. V. M. A. IVSTIN. Type of No. 713. Fair. 15. .35

725 —— *Aloys Mocenigo*, 1700-09. *Soldo*. S. M. V. ALOY. MOC. Type of No. 713. Good. 15. .30

726 —— Same. *Quattrino*. ALOY MOCENIGO DVX. A cross, surrounded by 12 pellets. *Rev.*, SANCTVS MARCVS VENETVS The winged lion of St. Mark boing the Book of the Evangelists. Fair. 12. .25

727 —— *Pietro Grimani*, 1741-52. *Soldo*. S. M. V. PIT GRIM D. Type of No. 713. Good. 15. .30

68

728 —— Republic. GOVERNO PROVVISORO DI VENEZIA. The winged lion of St. Mark, the head surrounded by a Nimbus, holding the Book of the Evangelists. In ex. the letters ZV. Beneath the ground upon which the lion sits the die-cutter's name, A FARRIN. *Rev.*, CENTESIMI | 5 | 1849 | DI LIRA CORRENTE. Good. .25
728*a* —— Same. 3 Centesimi. Good. .20
729 —— Same. 1 Centesimo. Good. .18
730 **Viterbo,** 2½ *Baiocchi.* S(anctus) P(etrus) APOSTOLORUM PRINCEPS. Bust of St. Peter l., the head surrounded by a Nimbus, holding the Keys of Heaven. *Rev.*, BAIOCCHI | DVE.E MEZZO | VITERBO | 1796. Fair. 20. .35
731 **Walthamstowe,** HALFPENNY. A lion advancing l. In ex. 1813. Britannia seated l., holding in her right hand an olive branch, her left supporting a shield and trident. Often classed with Canadian Tokens. Fine. 19. .25
732 **Warsaw.** A crowned shield of two parts between palm branches r. the Polish Eagle l. divided into 8 squares, 5 containing a leaf and pellets and 3 pellets alone. *Rev.*, 3 | GROSZE | 1812 | I. B. Fine. 17. .20
733 —— Type of last. *Rev.*, 1 | GROSZ | 1811 | I. S. Fine. 14. .15
734 **Zacatecas,** EST : LIBᴱ FED : DE ZACATECAS, 1863. A pyramid standing in a grove of 4 trees, a sacred grove of the Aztecs; against it stands an open book, the pages of which are inscribed : LEY. Above the book is a wreath, and at the base of the pyramid four others. In ex. Quartilla. *Rev.*, an angel, holding above its head a radiated liberty leaf upon an arrow, flying high above the city, the spires of which are dimly seen below. Brass. Fine. 18. .70
735 —— Type of last. 1827. *Octavo.* Brass. Fair. 14. .45
736 **Zamoscia,** Obsidional. PIENIA DZ | W. OBLEZENIU | ZAMOSCIA | 1813. *Rev.*, 6. | GROSZY. In ex. two palm branches crossed. Good. 21. 2.00
737 **Zellerfeld.** Mint-master's *Token.* I. B. HECHT. K. GR. BR. A. C. V. F. BR. LVN. MVNTZ-MEISTER Z(u) Z(ellerfeld). *Rev.*, DEO DVCET. Fair 17. .18
738 —— Same. HENNING SCHLUTER, F. R. L. M. M. Z. Z(ellerfeld). A shield of two parts within an ornament. r. a key. l. 3 bars. Above the shield 3 keys crossed within two eagles' wings. *Rev.*, CONSIDERA NOVISSIMA ET NON PECCARIS (Consider thy end and sin no more). A skull, from the openings of which worms are issuing. Behind, a scythe and a grave-digger's spade. Above, an hour-glass. Fine. 16. .25
739 **Zator,** *Maria Theresa.* A small crowned shield within a larger one also crowned. *Rev.*, 1 | SCHILLING | 1774 | S(chmolnitz). Poor. 12. .18
740 **Zutphen,** *Stuber.* MONETA VET. VRBIS. Crowned lion rampant l. *Rev.*, ZVTP | HANIEN | SIS. Fair. 14. .30
741 **Zurich.** CANTON ZURICH. A shield in form of a spade, divided into two parts. Upper, plain; lower, a scroll-like ornament. On either side oak and laurel branches. In ex. D. *Rev.*, 2 | RAPPEN | 1842. Base. Fine. 12. .18
742 **Zierikzee,** (Holland. Lion rampant l. Within an ornamental shield above. A small globe behind a cross. *Rev.*, 3 ST.(uber) | S(enatus) P(opulus) Q | ue) Z(ierikzee) | 1585. Brass. Fair. 16. 1.00

# COINS AND MEDALS.

THE FOLLOWING COINS AND MEDALS ARE IN
STOCK AND FOR SALE AT REASONABLE
PRICES.

Greek, Silver and Copper Coins of Cities and Princes.

Roman, Family and Imperial Denarii.

Roman 1st, 2d and 3d Brass.

American Colonial and U. S. Coins.

Small Proof Sets, Colonial and Fractional Currency and
Confederate Notes and Bonds.

Foreign Silver and Base Coins.

Foreign Copper in great variety. Specialty made in lots
of 50 and upwards at 3, 5, 7 and 10 cents each, none pierced
or worn smooth.

Tokens of Counties, Cities, Corporations and Merchants
of all Countries, 17th, 18th and 19th Centuries.

Silver and Bronze Medals of Illustrious Personages.

War Medals, Proclamation Pieces, Military Decorations
and Medals commemorative of Masonic Convocations.

White-metal Medals of Centennial, Bi-centennial and Tri-
ennial Celebrations, etc.; among which may be mentioned
the recent issues of Louisville, Denver (G.A.R.), German-
town (2 varieties), Newburg (2 varieties), Chicago, Worces-
ter, Santa Fé, Springfield, Newark, New York Evacuation
(8 varieties), Brooklyn Bridge (3 varieties), Martin Luther,
etc., etc.

Catalogues of American Coin Sales, past and present, also
a well-selected stock of valuable foreign.

www.ingramcontent.com/pod-product-compliance
Lightning Source LLC
Chambersburg PA
CBHW021449090426
42739CB00009B/1690